Create a
Growth
Mindset
School

Create a
Growth
Mindset
School

An Administrator's Guide to Leading a Growth Mindset Community

Mary Cay Ricci

PRUFROCK PRESS INC.
WACO, TEXAS

Library of Congress catalog information
currently on file with the publisher.

Copyright ©2018, Prufrock Press Inc.

Edited by Stephanie McCauley

Cover design by Micah Benson and layout design by Allegra Denbo

ISBN-13: 978-1-61821-783-7

Printed in the United States of America.

At the time of this book's publication, all facts and figures cited are the most current
available. All telephone numbers, addresses, and website URLs are accurate and active. All
publications, organizations, websites, and other resources exist as described in the book,
and all have been verified. The author and Prufrock Press Inc. make no warranty or guar-
antee concerning the information and materials given out by organizations or content
found at websites, and we are not responsible for any changes that occur after this book's
publication. If you find an error, please contact Prufrock Press Inc.

Prufrock Press Inc.
P.O. Box 8813
Waco, TX 76714-8813
Phone: (800) 998-2208
Fax: (800) 240-0333
http://www.prufrock.com

Table of Contents

CHAPTER 1
Leading With a Growth Mindset 1

CHAPTER 2
Reflecting on Your Mindset 7

CHAPTER 3
Leading With Optimism 21

CHAPTER 4
Deliberate Cultivation of Perseverance and Resiliency 31

CHAPTER 5
Praise and Feedback 43

CHAPTER 6
Setting the Stage for Professional Learning...................... 49

CHAPTER 7
Procedures and Policies to Promote
a Growth Mindset Environment.................................. 61

CHAPTER 8
Parent and Community Involvement 77

CHAPTER 9
Curriculum and Instruction 85

CHAPTER 10
A Growth Mindset School District 97

CHAPTER 11
Final Thoughts 109

References 115

APPENDIX A
Administrator's Mindset Reflection Tool: Answer Key.......... 119

APPENDIX B
Planning for Students' Unmet Academic Needs................ 125

APPENDIX C
Introducing Neuroscience in the Classroom.................... 129

About the Author 131

CHAPTER 1

Leading With a Growth Mindset

> Imagine a learning community where expectations are high for staff and students, optimism is palpable, mistakes are expected, struggle is embraced, equitable access to advanced learning is the norm, perseverance and resiliency are valued, and growth is the focus, not grades . . . a safe place where ideas are welcomed without judgment, adults and students persevere when facing barriers, and all educators believe that all students (and teachers) can be successful.

The school community that is described above is one where both adults and children apply a growth mindset—the belief that intelligence, talents, and skills are malleable and can be developed. The idea that intelligence can grow and improve in both children and adults has seen more popularity in recent years thanks to the work of Stanford University professor of psychology Dr. Carol Dweck. Her research and development of the fixed and growth mindset theory has also contributed to a major shift in thinking about administrator and teacher expectations, student learning, and intelligence.

Dweck (2006) described a belief system that asserts that intelligence and talent are malleable and can be developed—she coined the term *growth mindset* to describe this belief system. Learners with a growth mindset believe that with perseverance, resiliency, and the appropriate strategies, they can learn and improve. It might take some struggle, mistakes, and failure along the way, but they understand that with focused perseverance and resiliency, they can succeed. The focus of growth mindset thinking is on the process of learning, not on the final outcome or grade. An educator with a growth mindset believes that with effort, hard work, and application of strategies, all students can demonstrate significant growth, and therefore, all students deserve challenging instructional opportunities. Add to this belief an effective teacher armed with instructional tools that differentiate, respond to learners' needs, and nurture critical thinking processes, and you have a recipe for optimum student learning.

growth mindset

a belief system that suggests that one's intelligence, skills, and talents can be grown or developed with perseverance, resiliency, and application of appropriate strategies

Dweck (2006) also presented a different belief system about intelligence—a *fixed mindset*. A fixed mindset is the belief that intelligence, skills, and talents are things you are born with; they have a genetic component; and your level of intelligence and talents cannot be changed. A person with a fixed mindset might truly believe that he has a predetermined amount of intelligence, skills, or talents. This belief system is problematic for our students at both ends of the continuum. For those students who are not performing at grade level or do not perceive themselves as "smart," a fixed mindset becomes a self-fulfilling prophecy; because these students don't really believe that they can be successful, they will often give up and not put forth effort. For those students who are advanced learners, a fixed mindset can lead them to be consumed with "looking smart" at all costs. They may coast through school without really putting forth much effort, yet they are often praised for their good "work," grades, and strong skills. Often, an advanced learner with a fixed mindset will start avoiding situations where she may fail; she can become "risk averse."

fixed mindset

a belief system that suggests that a person has a predetermined amount of intelligence, skills, or talents

Think about your own mindset. Your mindset refers to your personal beliefs and thinking that influence your behavior and attitude toward yourself and others. Your mindset directly influences how your team feels about the school or office culture and how they view themselves as part of the school or office. An educator's mindset directly influences how children feel about themselves and how they view themselves as learners. A child's mindset directly affects how he or she faces academic challenges. A child with a growth mindset perseveres even in the face of barriers. A child with a fixed mindset may give up easily, lack resiliency, and not engage in the learning process. Believing that all adults and children can succeed, with effort, perseverance, resiliency, and effective strategies, is the heart of a growth mindset belief.

Why Lead With a Growth Mindset?

As education leaders, we make a lot of decisions every day: budgets, student placement, curriculum/instruction, behavior and intervention, etc. By the end of this book, you will be ready to make these everyday decisions through a growth mindset lens, which will contribute to an environment of growth in your school or office.

The Wallace Foundation (2013) identified key practices that effective education leaders do well in its report *The School Principal as Leader: Guiding Schools to Better Teaching and Learning.* The first (and, I would argue, the most important) of these practices is:

> Shaping a vision of academic success for all students. (p. 4)

This practice requires a growth mindset from everyone in a school building, not just leadership. Porter et al. (2008) from Vanderbilt University asserted,

> The research literature over the last quarter century has consistently supported the notion that having high expectations for all, including clear and public standards, is one key to closing the achievement gap between advantaged and less advantaged students and for raising the overall achievement of all students. (p. 13)

Effective education leaders work to establish a community-wide vision of commitment to high expectations and the success of all students. This is particularly important as we address both the achievement and opportunity gap. Leaders have tried countless ways to accomplish this goal with varying levels of success. But there *is* a way to accomplish this goal: Build a growth mindset learning community!

Discussion Questions

> Shaping a vision of academic success for all students is a key practice for education administrators. What does this practice have to do with a growth mindset?

> How might growth mindset thinking contribute to closing the achievement gap between advantaged and less advantaged children?

CHAPTER 2

Reflecting on Your Mindset

During my 28 years as an educator, I have never observed such rapid, sustainably impacting change as that experienced during our student, staff, and parent journey with growth mindset. The positive energy and shift in perspective experienced in our focus to praise effort and hard work and to view situations through the lens of the power of yet have been life-changing for our stakeholders. Both staff and parents have shared personal stories about the impact of understanding the difference between fixed and growth mindset. Growth mindset is not just another initiative, it's truly a change in thinking that shifts culture—it's a way of being!

—Kimberlyn Pratesi, Principal,
Hammond Elementary School, Howard County, MD

The first step in the journey toward a growth mindset learning community is to take time to really reflect on your own belief system about intelligence and academic talent. The superintendent sets the tone for the school district; central office administrators influence the tone of curriculum, instruction, and the interworking of the district; and the principal sets the tone for his or her school. Administrators' values, actions, and attitudes significantly impact the culture of the community. We all recognize it when people talk the talk but don't walk the walk. We may state that we have a growth mindset in our role as a leader, but our actions may demonstrate fixed mindset thinking.

The Administrator's Mindset Reflection Tool (see Figure 1) can help you examine your own mindset thinking. The intention of this tool is not to make you feel that your beliefs are being questioned, but simply to suggest where your reactions might lie based on various situations: growth mindset, fixed mindset, or somewhere in the middle. If you have never experienced the described situations in the survey, you may gravitate toward a growth mindset response, given what you have already learned about so far—or you might predict the reaction that you would like to have.

During a quiet time, reflect on the questions and statements. Don't think about what the "right" answer is—if none of the responses reflect how you would react, choose the one that is closest to your reaction or just skip it. I purposely have not asked you to calculate a score and find out if you are a fixed or growth mindset administrator. Why? Because there really isn't any such thing as a growth mindset person or a fixed mindset person. Mindsets come into play based on the situation that you are in—in a variety of situations, you either believe that, with perseverance, some mistakes along the way, and the right set of strategies, achievement will occur, or you believe that some people are not born with the capacity or ability to achieve in a particular area. You can compare your responses to the reflective explanations in Appendix A.

Administrator's Mindset Reflection Tool

1. You are observing a math class and are happy to see small-group instruction. As you circulate through the room, you see the teacher working with a group of struggling math students. You notice that the teacher jumps in to support each student as soon as he or she gets stuck. What are you thinking?
    a. I really like how this teacher is providing individual help for these students as soon as they need it.
    b. I wish she would let them struggle a bit more before helping them.
    c. I wonder why these students are behind the rest of the class. I need to set up a meeting to discuss.

2. During a preservice day, you are leading a staff meeting to discuss some new initiatives that the district has mandated. What do you do?
    a. Come prepared to the meeting with an implementation plan.
    b. Encourage staff to ask questions, contribute ideas, and participate in the development of the plan.
    c. Let staff know that these initiatives were not your idea, but central office says that they need to be implemented, so you will all work together to make sure that happens.

3. At each grade level in your school you have a special class or group for gifted learners. A teacher comes to you advocating for a child to join the group even though the child has not met the testing and report card grade criteria. How do you respond?
    a. I am sorry, but if I let him in, I will be setting a precedent for others. Can you imagine what parents would do if they found out?
    b. No, he will slow the other kids down.
    c. We have the criteria in place for a reason, and he did not meet the criteria.
    d. Let's give him a trial period of 6 weeks and see how he does.

FIGURE 1. Administrator's mindset reflection tool.

4. Do you believe that all educators can develop their teaching skills with practice and effort from the teacher and support and feedback from an instructional coach?
   a. Yes
   b. No

5. Every year each administrator receives feedback from the educators and staff who are part of his or her team. You recently reviewed the feedback and noticed that several people had concerns about you in the following areas: listening without interrupting and micromanaging their work. How do you respond?
   a. Well, I am responsible for what happens in this building/office, and I am sorry that they consider that micromanaging.
   b. These comments are probably from the people that I have had concerns with—sour grapes!
   c. I really need to work on letting people speak first before I interrupt. I also need to work on backing off my staff . . . I know they have the capacity and expertise to do their job.

6. Do you provide specific feedback to teachers outside of evaluations or formal visits?
   a. Always
   b. Occasionally
   c. Not often/Never

7. A teacher approaches you and asks if he can attend a conference focused on ways to embed technology into instruction. He states that he will pay for the conference himself but would like to have approval to attend, and requests that he does not have to use his sick leave if at all possible. What do you think?
   a. He just wants to get away. He will never implement anything that he learns.
   b. I am so glad that he is seeking new ways to use technology in his classroom. I will ask him to share what he learns when he returns and find a way that he will not have to use sick leave.
   c. The conference looks great. I wonder if I can attend and send a few more teachers as well.

FIGURE 1. Continued.

There are likely areas of administration where you tend to have more of a growth mindset and other areas where you tend to have a fixed mindset. The following example shows how education leaders may use different mindsets in different situations.

Mr. Smith had been the principal of a K–8 school for 5 years when he learned that the school district would be using a brand-new data management system. Mr. Smith immediately applied fixed mindset thinking to the situation. He thought,

> Oh no, it took me about three years to learn everything that the last system could do—I will never get the hang of a new system . . . I need to ask my assistant principal (or resource teacher, secretary, etc.) to learn this. Then he (or she) can run the data reports for me.

Mr. Smith's response to a new data management system shows how fixed mindset thinking is often applied to new challenges.

Now let's think about Mr. Smith in a different situation. During his daily classroom walkthroughs, he noticed that one of his new teachers, Mr. Matthews, appeared to be struggling with classroom management. He scheduled a meeting with him and learned that Mr. Matthews was open to all of the suggestions that Mr. Smith had to help with management. Mr. Smith let Mr. Matthews know that he was confident that the management would improve once he got some practice and strategies under his belt. About a week later Mr. Smith noticed some improvement. He left a note on Mr. Matthews's desk that said, "I can see the effort that you have put forth, and it really shows! Your behavior management is not quite there yet, but with some more practice being consistent, you will get there!"

Mr. Smith applied fixed mindset thinking to one situation and growth mindset thinking to another in his role as a principal. The ideal approach, of course, would be to apply growth mindset thinking across all aspects of his job as an administrator.

The results of the Administrator's Mindset Reflection Tool suggest the way your mindset leans at this moment in time. Mindsets can change—with deliberate practice and effort. If you have discovered that you lean toward growth mindset thinking, focus on the items where your thinking leans toward fixed or is in the middle. You might be thinking, "I didn't realize that I actually lean toward growth mindset thinking," or "I thought I had a growth mindset, but my responses lean more toward fixed." The purpose of this short reflection is to help you tune into your own mindset in relation to situations that you might encounter as a principal or central office leader. If you have discovered that you lean toward fixed mindset thinking, think about how you might shift responses and reactions in specific areas.

Why is it important to have a solid understanding of your own mindset beliefs before embarking on building a growth mindset learning community? According to Tschannen-Moran (2014),

> Discontinuity between word and deed will quickly erode a principal's ability to lead. Setting a positive example is not a task to be flaunted by principals, however; it is more a matter of leading *quietly* to earn the trust and cooperation of faculty. (p. 256)

This need for trust and cooperation applies to both school and district leadership. You must fully understand what it means to lead with a growth mindset, or you may not be taken seriously. School and district leaders who apply growth mindset thinking have the opportunity to empower all educators and students. Our children deserve teachers and administrators who model growth mindset thinking each day.

Consider how you might approach the following scenario.

Two days before the start of the school year, Mrs. Wilson, a high school principal, is approached by an 11th-grade student, Mia, who wants to enroll in an honors science course. Mia has already spoken to her counselor and the department head, who told her that the school has specific criteria (grades and test scores) for participation in honors courses and she does not meet those criteria. Mia asks Mrs. Wilson if she has a few minutes to talk with her, and they proceed to the conference room. Mia shares that she had an opportunity during the summer to volunteer at a summer camp where the focus was science, and it really piqued her interest. She developed an interest in biology, particularly genetics. She continues to advocate for enrollment in an honors biology course by explaining to Mrs. Wilson that she has since learned a lot more due to further reading and watching of online videos about biology and genetics. Mia explains that she would have some knowledge going into the course. She adds that she is willing to work very hard and stay after school for extra help if she needs to.

Mia's background to consider:
> Her grades range from A's to D's.
> Her attendance history is good.
> Her standardized test scores are in the average range.

Think about the following questions:
1. If you were Mrs. Wilson, what are some things that you would be thinking?
2. Other than grades, attendance, and test scores, is there anything else that should be considered?
3. Would you allow Mia to enroll in the honors course? Why or why not?

We will come back to these questions later on. Let's learn a little bit more about intelligence.

We Can All Get Smarter

Research over the last several years has contributed to the understanding of malleable intelligence, a key factor in growth mindset and a concept some educators question. In general, educators do not have a lot of background in cognitive science. I asked several groups of educators the following question: "What do cognitive abilities tests/IQ tests measure?" Without exception, there was hesitancy in responding to the question; after I had given sufficient wait time, a few responses were shared: "a child's capability," "how smart they are," and "their innate ability." What surprised me more than their responses was the observation that so many of these teachers and administrators just could not answer the question. There are many times when educators are in situations where data is shared about a student, and that data often includes cognitive scores from gifted and talented screening processes, special education screening processes, and/or IQ tests. Who knew so many educators really have no idea what these assessments actually measure?

Cognitive ability assessments measure *developed* ability. Therefore, if a child has never had an opportunity to develop the kinds of reasoning processes that these assessments measure, the outcome of one of these assessments would not be meaningful. David Lohman (2004), professor of educational psychology at the University of Iowa and cocreator of the Cognitive Abilities Test (CogAT), stated that abilities are developed through experiences in school and outside of school. When parents and educators review these "intelligence" scores, assumptions may be made about the child, and beliefs may kick in that place limits on the child's potential.

I would bet you have heard an adult or student say something like, "I am just not a math person." Perhaps you have said it yourself (I have!). Jo Boaler's 2016 book, *Mathematical Mindsets: Unleashing Students' Potential Through Creative Math, Inspiring Messages and Innovative Teaching* discussed the myth of the "mathematically gifted child." Boaler pointed out that problems can arise from a "pervasive idea that 'math people' are those born with something different" (p. 94). She continued, "Add to this idea the stereotyped notions about who is 'naturally' good at math, and we start to understand the nature of the problem that we face" (p. 94). She explained that part of the problem is math inequality. We tend to have stereotyped notions about who is good in math and who is not. This mindset about math is fixed—believing that there are "math people" and "not math people" perpetuates fixed mindset thinking and allows an "out" for students who believe that they don't have the innate ability to understand math. An elementary school principal shared with me that the only challenge that she faced as she built a growth mindset school was a teacher who claimed that she was a terrible math student and, therefore, she could not teach math. This claim is a perfect example of fixed mindset thinking.

Intelligence, skills, and talents can grow. Many educators are unaware that approximately 75% of achievement is attributed to psychosocial skills (which can also be referred to as noncognitive factors) and only approximately 25% is attributed to innate intelligence or IQ (Olszewski-Kubilius, 2013). The cultivation of noncognitive skills is imperative, especially for those students who have not yet developed their abilities and/or talents. The skills that must be deliberately modeled, taught, and cultivated include but are not limited to: perseverance, resiliency, grit, comfort with intellectual tension, and the ability to handle critique and constructive feedback.

Think about a student who has strong innate abilities—she learns quickly and gives correct responses in class. What if this student lacks perseverance and academic resiliency? As soon as things get challenging or she is not finding success easily, she disengages. It will not matter how strong any innate abilities are if she has not developed perseverance and academic resiliency; her achievement will suffer. The opposite is also true—think of a student whose innate abilities, according to a test, are "average" (I really do not like using this word but am doing so for illustrative purposes), but he shows strength in perseverance and resiliency.

This student may be able to work side by side with those students whose innate abilities are stronger because he has the motivation and has developed important noncognitive skills in order to stick with and embrace challenge.

Now, apply this thinking to teachers, aides, and paraeducators in a school. Picture a teacher who has high expectations, solid classroom management, and good rapport with her students, but lacks perseverance. She may engage students in a powerful learning experience but does not have the persistence to circle back around and work with students who are not grasping the concept the first time around. She charges ahead, teaching standards without always assessing formatively. When she does use formative assessment, she does not use the information to adjust her delivery or to reteach.

The same thinking may occur in the central office—you may have a team member who brings great ideas to the table but lacks the tenacity or resiliency to follow through with implementation. By focusing on perseverance and resiliency as an office goal and providing support, central office staff can develop these skills as well.

Think of a time when it took you a little longer to learn a new skill. It may have been something that required physical coordination, playing a musical instrument, or using a new observation and evaluation platform. Then, once you learned this new skill, it became a strength area for you. In fact, you surpassed many others who had this skill for much longer than you did. As an adult, you had the drive, motivation, and persistence to decide that reaching this goal was important to you. No one took away the opportunity to let you learn, no one told you it was "too hard" for you, and no one told you that this was "not the right group" for you. No one put up barriers to hinder your learning.

Yet, there are times when our education system does all of the above. Many of our school practices and policies eliminate opportunities, communicate low expectations, and prematurely remove students from challenging environments. Many reasons exist for hampering student potential in this way; one major obstacle is how we judge both adults and children by the speed at which they complete tasks.

Our society has become one that values pace. The faster, the better. If we don't get our large, decaf, skim, extra hot, caramel latte in less than 2 minutes, then we are annoyed. If our Internet connection is not instant, then we grumble or click fast and furiously. If a driver in front of us is not going at a pace we agree with, then we use the horn or moan out loud. If an educator describes a bright child in his classroom or school, then we might hear him refer to the child as "quick" and those in the bottom reading group as "slow."

We need to step back, take a breath, and realize that it is not about how fast students master learning. It is about the perseverance and effort that they put forth and the strategies that they utilize.

Potential

Potential is a great word. It is all about possibilities. However, it is often used in ways that makes no sense. Think of the phrase, "He is not working to his full potential" or "We will help your child reach his or her full potential." (These phrases may even be on your school or district website.) How does potential become "full"? Is it something that can be checked off on a report card? Potential can never be "full"; it is never-ending, and our possibilities are infinite. As a person grows, learning and experiences become more complex and challenging, growth continually occurs, and potential is never reached because it is impossible to reach. Perhaps many thought Michael Phelps reached his "full" potential after earning his 16th Olympic medal in 2008—a feat he went on to shatter at the 2012 Olympics when he won six more medals, and an additional six in 2016. Believing that intelligence, talent, skills, and even musical, artistic, and athletic abilities can be developed encourages these endless possibilities. Our goal should be to provide both adults and children with opportunities to realize that we all have endless potential.

We are all born with potential in most areas. However, we might have innate strength or capacity in one or more specific areas. Strengths can be shown physically, creatively, socially, academically—the possibilities are endless. Every person has strengths, and some people are born with a greater degree of intrinsic strength in a particular area compared to members of their peer group. However, it is important to remember two things: (1) that even if we are born with intrinsic strength in an area, we still need to work to further develop that area, and (2) that other people who have developed important noncognitive skills have the potential to work side by side or even surpass those with intrinsic abilities.

Guiding school-based and district leaders on a path toward establishing a school or district community that promotes the belief that intelligence is malleable is one of the goals of this book. The entire school staff—administrators, teachers, and support staff—as well as parents must truly believe that all children can be successful. Children must also accept this belief. It is all about beliefs and expectations. One way to contribute greatly to both children and adults embracing this belief system is learning about the brain and all of its possibilities. Neuroscience has grown by leaps and bounds in the last several years, and educating ourselves and our students about the brain has a huge impact on understanding student learning, effort, and motivation. (See Appendix C for more information on teaching neuroscience and mindsets.)

Let's go back and think about Mia's self-advocacy for participation in Honors Biology (see p. 13). Did you immediately think of logistical issues, such as the following?

> › The course is already full—no room for another student.
> › If I let her in the class, then other students may want to get in the class as well.
> › Parents won't be happy if we don't stick with the criteria for class enrollment.

It sounds like Mia has the motivation to give Honors Biology a try, and isn't it our responsibility to allow access to challenging learning for our students? Does Mia have equitable access to advanced learning? Why is equitable access important? Do the criteria that have been established for entrance into advanced courses include a child's motivation, work ethic, or resiliency?

After much listening, observing, research, and reflection, I have identified four components that are essential to a growth mindset learning environment. These are areas that each learning environment should strive to obtain. These cannot happen overnight and sometimes not even within one school year. These actions should be a long-term commitment, and educators must have a growth mindset themselves in order to persevere to attain these goals. These four components are:

1. equitable access to advanced learning opportunities;
2. deliberate cultivation of psychosocial skills, such as perseverance, resiliency, and grit;
3. student understanding of neural networks in the brain; and
4. growth mindset feedback and praise.

The following chapters will address these components.

Discussion Questions

> Every person has a fixed mindset in some part of his or her life. What are some areas of your life, both professional and personal, where you demonstrate a fixed mindset?

> Does your district or school allow for students like Mia to access advanced coursework? If not, what policies could change?

CHAPTER 3

Leading With Optimism

Let's now focus on a very underrated but extremely important skill that is the foundation to any new initiative in any office or school building and is crucial in growth mindset work—optimism. Trying to see the best or what is good in every situation is optimism. In many work environments, there are people whom I refer to as "pot-stirrers" (those who tend to promote drama and may recruit others to join in). One goal in a growth mindset environment is to help those who have negative intentions to see the positive outcomes that are possible. After all, an ideal team would involve those who practice optimism. An optimistic person is a person with hope, and we all want our learning communities to be places of hope.

Can optimism be taught? Let's first think about the opposite of optimism—pessimism. Most of us have at least one pessimist in our lives. What happens if we spend too much time with a pessimist? We can pick up on the same behaviors! Pessimism is contagious—have you ever sat at a meeting or professional learning session when someone at the table starts complaining, "That will never work at my school," or "Here comes a new initiative that will disappear in a few months"? On many occasions, others at the table begin adopting the same pessimistic mindset. However, it *is* possible for a pessimist to become more optimistic. A pessimist can learn ways to adjust his or her thinking and internal dialogue to think more optimistically. A pessimist can learn to recognize some of the reasons why he or she is thinking negatively. Just as pessimism can be contagious, so can optimism. If a learning environment is predominantly optimistic, this outlook will contribute greatly to a growth mindset school.

An optimistic brain is a happy brain. Neuroscientists have discovered that consistent negative or positive thoughts and feelings can affect brain activity and have an impact on learning. You can train your brain to help you become a more optimistic person. Being an optimistic learner is beneficial for children and adults, as it helps them become ready to master new learning and be optimistic about their ability to do so. It just makes sense that a growth mindset school is an optimistic school.

Andrew Weil, a doctor and author of the 2011 book, *Spontaneous Happiness: A New Path to Emotional Well-Being*, pointed to studies showing that not only can intelligence be developed, but emotions, such as happiness and empathy, can be developed as well. In the same way that practice improves a singer's voice, an athlete's performance, or a mathematician's growth and development, practice can also help a person become happier. Weil cited studies of the brain organized by Richard Davidson, Director of the Laboratory for Affective Neuroscience at the University of Wisconsin-Madison, which showed that "there are no peaceful molecules without peaceful thoughts" (p. 65). Davidson performed brain scans on Matthieu Ricard, a French person who earned a doctorate in molecular genetics, then later became a Buddhist monk. Based on data Davidson collected, he dubbed Ricard "The World's Happiest Man." He found that Ricard had increased activity in the left prefrontal cortex of the brain, which is associated with positive emotions. Ricard makes an effort to be happy, practices happiness, and works to eliminate negative emotions through meditation—remember, he is now a Buddhist monk! This study demonstrates that happiness can be learned with deliberate practice.

As growth mindset leaders, we strive to be happy, empathetic, kind, and supportive. We want our team to feel happy, safe, and willing to take risks around us. Our "energy" is positive and likely contagious. A leader who applies growth mindset thinking to situations will radiate that positive energy to adults and children. Growth mindset leaders create supportive environments and understand how their actions directly influence school climate. They treat everyone with respect and kindness, engage positively with their team and students, and value positive relationships.

What About Venting?

Some organizations adopt a "no venting" zone, where the focus is on problem solving rather than venting about issues. Although I agree that collaborative problem solving is crucial, I question the "no venting" zone policy. Psychology tells us that positive venting can help reduce stress.

When we let problems affect us, and our emotions run high, our thought processes can become foggy. If you have someone to talk to whom you trust, you should go ahead and vent—as long as you are very careful about whom you decide to vent to. If this person is sympathetic, then you are likely to be able to think more clearly and your concerns will feel more legitimate. This makes the venting a positive experience. If the person hearing your concerns does not show empathy and support, then venting turns into a negative experience. It is also not a positive venting situation if someone is a serial venter—a person who vents to anyone and everyone he or she can find who will listen in order to gain sympathy, either for being a victim or to get others on his or her "side." This is when venting becomes negative and unhealthy.

Leon Seltzer (2014), a clinical psychologist and author, identified six virtues and vices of venting. (Read more by scanning the QR code to the right or visiting https://www.psychology today.com/blog/evolution-the-self/201404/6-virtues-and-6-vices-venting.) He really drove home the importance of choosing the right person to talk to. Seltzer stated:

> As long as you're sufficiently careful in selecting whom you'll confide in, their sympathetic response is likely to make you feel better—or at least not quite as bad. The troubling sense of being all alone in your misfortune is almost always significantly reduced by another's concerned willingness to allow you to share your grievances with them. Just in itself, self-expression feels good. But what can help you feel even better is being listened to by someone who genuinely seems to care about you. For through their warmheartedly "getting" your discomfiture and commiserating with you, your frustrations feel all the more rightful and legitimate. (para. 6)

Consider the following scenario.

After being in an administrator's position for just about a year, Mr. Miller was assigned a new director. He was perplexed about some shenanigans that were occurring between Ms. Jones, who was in the position prior to Mr. Miller's arrival, and current district staff. During a meeting with his new director, Ms. Black, he was asked if there were any issues that he would like to discuss. As Mr. Miller began to share the undermining that was taking place by Ms. Jones, Ms. Black immediately cut him off and shared that she did not have an interest in what Ms. Jones was up to. Neither did Mr. Miller, but the behaviors were getting in the way of important school and district initiatives.

Ms. Black did not give Mr. Miller a place to not only vent, but also share a plan to solve the issue. Although he was looking to inform her and let off some steam (after all, that is what venting does), more importantly, he was looking for a thought partner because the behaviors were affecting the education of students in the district. Ms. Black was not assuming positive intentions from Mr. Miller. Perhaps she thought he was there to complain; she did not allow a chance for collaborative problem solving . . . and maybe most importantly, she did not know him well and assumed he was there to throw the previous administrator under the bus.

Mr. Miller's new director did not give him what he needed as far as a sympathetic response. The director did not even allow an opportunity for him to finish speaking.

Think about the following questions:

> What might have been a productive response from the director, Ms. Black, if she had listened to Mr. Miller?
> Reflect on your beliefs about venting—as the person doing the venting as well as the person listening. How might your beliefs about venting affect your capacity to lead with optimism?
> Why is leading with optimism a critical part of a growth mindset learning community?

Optimistic School Culture

According to researcher Dana Lightman (2005), optimism can actually make you smarter. Lightman stated,

> An added plus in the workplace is the fact that optimism makes you smarter. Researchers have

shown that positive emotions actually fuel creativity and enhance your reasoning skills, creating more successful results. This is because a positive mood changes the way your brain processes information. If you're under stress, feel beaten down, or are in a sad mood, your brain hunkers down. You become more detached and cautious because your brain focuses on what's wrong and how to eliminate it. On the other hand, when you are in a relaxed, cheerful mood, your brain opens up. More neurons fire and your brain is likely to enter into a creative, exploratory state. You begin to seek out new experiences in your environment. You feel expansive, generous, tolerant and productive. (para. 4)

Lightman (2005) also pointed out that we can all develop the tools for a positive work environment by asking five questions that allow us to adapt to change in a more positive way:

1. What can I do to achieve the best possible outcome?
2. What are innovative responses to the situation?
3. What do I need to know to reach a productive conclusion?
4. What can I learn from this situation that will help me in the future?
5. What is an interpretation of this event that will motivate me to continue to strive for excellence and success? (para. 5)

By putting these questions into practice, we eventually learn to handle a variety of situations that arise. Focus on what you can control. Be creative, objective, and open. When you hit a barrier, reflect, regroup, and move forward. That's a growth mindset!

In *Deliberate Optimism: Reclaiming the Joy in Education*, authors Silver, Berckemeyer, and Baenen (2015) defined five principles of deliberate optimism (see Figure 2). Many times, we react in a pessimistic or negative way when we hear about things

1. Before acting or reacting, **gather as much information** from as many varied sources as possible.
2. **Determine what is beyond your control** and strategize how to minimize its impact on your life.
3. **Establish what you can control** and seek tools and strategies to help you maximize your power.
4. Actively **do** something positive toward your goal.
5. **Take ownership** of your plan and acknowledge responsibility for your choices.

FIGURE 2. Five principles of deliberate optimism [emphasis added]. From *Deliberate Optimism: Reclaiming the Joy in Education* (p. 7), by D. Silver, J. C. Berchemeyer, and J. Baenen, 2015, Thousand Oaks, CA: Corwin.

that might bring about change, observe something that creates an emotional reaction, or feel that an injustice has occurred. However, by using the five principles that the authors put forth, we can become more deliberate in our responses to a variety of situations.

Another vital component of an optimistic school culture is deliberately assuming positive intentions from each member of your team. We sometimes have individuals on our team who exude negative energy; they may feel that they are victims, gossip and complain about others, and display other pessimistic behaviors. Other members of your team may actually feel uncomfortable or unhappy around them. You yourself may be a leader who leans toward pessimistic thinking, or you may be viewed as someone with negative energy. In the article, "Understanding Positive and Negative Energy in People," Mindvalley (2018) provided guidelines to move from being a person who radiates negative energy to one who radiates positive energy. The suggestions put forth include the following:

› Do what makes you happy.
› Choose to see the good in people.
› Know that you are in control of your own energy.
› Talk about what can go right instead of what can go wrong.

These suggestions may be easier said than done. How can you become more optimistic? How can the people you lead become more optimistic?

Unfortunately, some people are content being negative and pessimistic. They rationalize the pessimism in a way so that they will not be disappointed if things don't go their way. In her book, *Rainy Brain, Sunny Brain*, psychologist Elaine Fox (2012) cited many brain studies that support the malleability of our brains and ways we can retrain our brains to become happier and more optimistic. She cited psychologist Barbara Frederickson, who is an advocate for bringing positive emotions into our lives. Frederickson found that we all need a 3 to 1 ratio in our lives, meaning three positive emotions for every one negative emotion (p. 195). These positive emotions can include compassion, contentment, hope, love, and gratitude. Negative emotions include fear, shame, sadness, embarrassment, and anger. In order to be at our best, we don't have to eliminate all negative emotions; we just need to keep tabs on that 3 to 1 ratio.

Consider the following scenario.

At one of the first staff meetings that Mrs. Thomas held, she shared with her new team that a positive, optimistic work environment was important to her as a leader. She wanted the environment to not only be a place where people looked forward to going to work every day, but also a place where collaboration was the norm. She expected a good work ethic while at work, but expected staff to prioritize family at home. She asked the team to work toward a balance between work and home. She shared that she had an open-door policy (unless the office door was closed) if anyone wanted to speak with her. Honesty, trust, optimism, collaboration, and transparency would be the hallmarks of her leadership.

What Mrs. Thomas underestimated were the actions and behaviors that a few team members were accustomed to prior to her arrival. One team member, Doris, always looked as though she had the weight of the world on her shoulders—she never smiled, did not participate in team discussions, and radiated negative energy. Mrs. Thomas's plan was to slowly build a positive, trusting relationship with Doris that would enable Mrs. Thomas to learn more about her and mentor her. However, what really challenged her was another team member, Denise, who had a pessimistic outlook and used every excuse she could to get out of work: illness, car trouble, home repairs, you name it. Denise even falsely accused a fellow staff member of theft to get out of work. How should Mrs. Thomas approach this issue?

It is likely that Mrs. Thomas will not be able to change the behaviors of Denise, who lacks work ethic and optimism. Mrs. Thomas can try to mentor her, provide ongoing feedback, and set goals with her. However, she may not be able to help Denise make the changes that need to be made. In these instances, administrators need to document absences, behaviors, and quality of work to eventually have the staff member removed from the school or office. Although a growth mindset community encourages support and growth, we should not keep staff who are not positive and productive team members.

Finally, to inspire optimism in your school, look at leaders outside of the realm of education. Warren Buffett, investor and philanthropist, models optimism in all he does. It is optimism that drives his success; he is not optimistic because of his success. Bill Gates, principal founder of Microsoft, and his wife, philanthropist Melinda Gates, summarized optimism in a way that we should all remember, stating, "Optimism isn't a belief that things will automatically get better; it's a conviction that we can make things better" (Clifford, 2017). As education leaders, we share that conviction—we can make things better.

Discussion Questions

> Why is an optimistic environment important in a school or district striving to become a place where growth mindset principles are at its core?

> What is one change that you could make to contribute to a more optimistic culture?

CHAPTER 4

Deliberate Cultivation of Perseverance and Resiliency

Promoting the importance of developing perseverance, resiliency, and grit, which are all part of learning from mistakes and failure, should be woven into your mission and vision. The cultivation of noncognitive/psychosocial skills is imperative, for both the students who have not yet developed their abilities and/or talents and high-performing students. If I had to narrow down the most important skills that must be deliberately modeled, taught, and cultivated, I would select perseverance and academic resiliency. We have students who demonstrate resiliency at home due to a challenging home environment, or on the field when playing sports they enjoy, but these demonstrations of resiliency do not easily translate into academics. Development of these psychosocial skills should be part of the climate of the district, school, and classroom; discussed across every content area; and modeled daily by the entire school community.

Students can self-evaluate and make plans for improving and tracking their growth in these skills. They can make a conscious effort to improve their ability to bounce back after a less-than-successful performance or failure to master a new concept. They can also anticipate barriers before beginning complex assignments or projects. Teachers can ask students to respond to these questions before they begin:

> Is there anything that concerns you about the task?
> How will you handle any of these concerns or obstacles that might get in your way?

Students can then begin working toward being diligent about their actions.

A recommended first step in deliberate cultivation of psychosocial skills is to reflect upon what is already in place in your school or district. Take some time with your staff to think about what is happening right now—those programs and actions already in place that cultivate skills like perseverance and resiliency. Perhaps you can create a shared document to send to your team for input. If you are a central office administrator, perhaps the document would include items such as those found in Table 1. A school's document might look something like Table 2. After collecting this information on a shared document, have a discussion at your next staff meeting about what was shared. Add to and edit the document. Then reflect and make a plan for ways to further cultivate these skills and to monitor or measure progress.

You may decide to begin this discussion face-to-face rather than using a shared document. At a staff meeting, capture this information together through a discussion. If you are school-based, be sure to include building service workers, paraeducators (aides), cafeteria workers, etc. It is important that everyone is part of this planning. My suggestion is to focus on only perseverance and resiliency at the elementary level; for middle and high school students and educators, you can add the concept of grit. Brainstorm together about schoolwide or districtwide experiences that will deliberately cultivate these noncognitive skills.

TABLE 1

Administrator's Psychosocial Skills Reflection

Psychosocial skill (noncognitive)	Practices in place that cultivate the skill	Ideas that would further develop the skill	Ideas for measuring progress in this area
Perseverance	Grade 6 middle school transition course includes a growth mindset unit.	Curriculum/English language arts office will identify and highlight books in the curriculum that feature literary characters who demonstrate perseverance. Science/social studies/STEM team will identify people who contributed to their fields who demonstrated perseverance. This will be an enrichment path that teachers can access.	Set up quarterly executive staff meetings to reflect on how the central office is supporting schools in building a growth mindset learning community.
Resiliency	Same as above.	Counseling staff will develop lessons focused on resiliency.	Same as above.

TABLE 2
Schoolwide Psychosocial Skills Reflection

Psychosocial skill (noncognitive)	Practices in place that cultivate the skill	Ideas that would further develop the skill	Ideas for measuring progress in this area
Perseverance	Students and teachers/support staff who go above and beyond in demonstrating perseverance are recognized with a shout-out on morning announcements.	School counselors or student advisors will do weekly growth mindset lessons focusing on perseverance and resiliency. Schoolwide assemblies could focus on perseverance. Grade-level or content-area teams will identify a video or a piece of text to use each week that will elicit a discussion about perseverance, resiliency, or growth mindset.	Students will self-evaluate each quarter using a district- or school-created electronic survey. Teachers will identify a few students who give up easily and maintain anecdotal records that will capture their growth in persevering.
Resiliency	None (yet!)	Students and teachers/support staff who go above and beyond in demonstrating resiliency will be recognized with a shout-out on morning announcements.	Students will self-evaluate each quarter using a district- or school-created electronic survey.

Establish Look Fors (student and teacher behaviors that you will observe when you walk through any room in the school building; see Chapter 11 for examples) and a plan for monitoring (not grading) student progress over time in the areas of concentration.

Learning From Failure

Hand in hand with nurturing perseverance and resiliency is teaching students how to learn from errors and failure. Mistakes should be considered "data"—this data can help a student set goals for moving toward understanding. The atmosphere of your school or district should be one where mistakes and failures are viewed as just part of the learning process. Learning occurs for all of us when we are stretched just beyond our typical comfort zone. Provide opportunities for your team to make mistakes, reflect, and try again. In order for our teachers to help kids get comfortable with mistakes, they must be comfortable as well, and as a leader, you must react to errors and mistakes in a way that models this thinking. I have found that the use of new technology for teachers and central office staff can provide a great opportunity for educators to attempt new learning that may not be in their comfort zone, make mistakes, learn, practice, and eventually have success.

Tom Kelley and David Kelley (2013), authors of *Creative Confidence: Unleashing the Creative Potential Within Us All*, recommended that we embrace our failures and own them. If we don't reflect on our failures and really figure out what went wrong, we will not know how to improve the outcome the next time. As they shared, "Acknowledging mistakes is also important for moving on. In doing so, you not only sidestep the psychological pitfalls of cover-up, rationalization, and guilt: you may also find that you enhance your own brand through your honesty, candor, and humility" (p. 51).

Here are some ways that you can model this concept:

> Share some of your favorite, most epic mistakes with staff or students. Then share what you learned from these mistakes.

> Encourage staff or students to share some of their mistakes or failures and what they learned from them.

> When you make a mistake, admit it and share what was learned and how you will move forward.

> Create a safe environment where no one makes fun of or comments on someone else's error in a negative way.

When learning from mistakes and failure, it is important to know how to give and receive constructive, specific feedback without taking it personally. The video "Austin's Butterfly: Building Excellence in Student Work" (available at https://vimeo.com/38247060) is good viewing not only for teacher professional learning, but also for students in all grades. The video clearly demonstrates how feedback and critique can improve an outcome *if* students are given opportunities to work on, practice, and improve their work.

When we consistently provide challenging opportunities for students, we find that students react to challenges in different ways. Some students have a "bring it on" approach and embrace each challenge with enthusiasm. Many of these students acknowledge that they may not be successful and may even fail at a task or two, but they want to take the risk. Other students feel threatened by the challenge, are afraid that they will not succeed, and will often give up before they put forth too much effort. It is imperative that leaders develop a school climate where failure is viewed as an expected and very important part of the learning process and students learn to reflect and redirect so that they can approach a challenging task in a new way or with more effort.

Allowing Redos and Retakes

A few years ago I was having a conversation with my 12th-grade daughter about failure. She shared that many teachers in her elementary, middle, and high schools would say things to the class like, "It's OK to make mistakes in our class—as long as we learn from them." It was a sentiment that sounded good to me—until she shared that no support ever existed to help figure out why the mistakes happened. The teachers also made sure the students knew that "every grade counts." Her point? If a teacher truly believes that mistakes are OK, then he or she should have structures in place that support students and guide them in reflecting and analyzing what went wrong. Additionally, the grades that "count" should be the versions that show understanding.

Allow students to redo assignments and retake assessments only if structures are in place that will help them learn the information in a new way or practice and apply the information. There is no sense in doing something over again if no reflection or new learning has taken place. A math teacher might allow a test retake if a score is below a certain grade—however, this is not helpful if no systematic support is given before the retake. As my daughter said, teachers often tell students, "Go over in that corner (or come in at recess or after school) to retake your test"—with no additional instruction, support, or guidance. If a teacher truly believes in the importance of errors as a learning device, and students are trying to learn from mistakes, then don't give a grade on the student's first try. Work with the student and guide him or her to approach the learning in a new way, and always provide a time and space for practice. For more discussion about redos and retakes, see Chapter 7.

Embrace the Struggle

In order for students to build resiliency and perseverance, they must have opportunities to struggle. Too many times I have heard administrators and teachers say things like, "Oh, I don't want him to struggle," or "I want all of my students to have success with this assignment." This thinking can be a huge disservice to our students. We cannot build academic resiliency if students are underchallenged. At the secondary level, we often put up barriers and do not allow equitable access to honors, Advanced Placement (AP), and International Baccalaureate (IB) courses, or if we do allow access, we don't provide the extra support that will allow students to struggle toward understanding and success. For more guidance on determining students' unmet academic needs, please see Appendix B.

The following are a few examples of the support we can give struggling students:

> Make sure they have a solid understanding of growth mindsets!

> Make sure they have go-to strategies that will help them when they are stuck.

> Offer before and/or afterschool time for questions and/or reteaching.

> Create small groups within the class that can work with the teacher to clarify confusing concepts.

> Offer study groups or one-on-one tutoring led by students who successfully took the course. (This tutoring could count as service hours for the leaders.)

A misunderstanding of struggle is widespread among educators. For example, recently I was meeting with a middle school principal to discuss her plan to make growth mindset thinking front and center at her school. As I was putting forth some ideas for future professional learning sessions, she leaned forward and said in almost a whisper, "Please don't use that word." I was puzzled and asked which word she was referring to. Her reply: "Struggle . . . it's such a negative word." That single sentence provided so much insight into the way many educators view struggle. Struggling is not a bad thing. If we are struggling, we are learning. Educators and students can get to a place where they enjoy the struggle. Think for a minute about the games we play on our phones and computers. Why do we spend time playing these games? We don't get a check in the mail or our names in the paper. We play them because we like the challenge, the struggle of getting to the next level or beating our previous time. Our brains actually reward us by releasing dopamine, which is one of the reasons we continue to play these games (Smith, 2014, para. 4). This leaves us with a great feeling after we have struggled through something and eventually found success. Many of our students never get an opportunity to get that great feeling because they are consistently underchallenged.

One issue I have observed is that sometimes counselors will counsel kids out of hard courses or not question a student when he or she wants to drop an accelerated course. Consider the following example.

> High school student William was enrolled in an Advanced Placement class. Prior to taking this class, coursework had been easy for him and he did not have to put forth a whole lot of effort. After a few weeks in the course, William began to struggle. He met with his counselor to see if he could be switched to a non-AP section. Instead of agreeing to his request, his counselor encouraged him to work through the struggle—she talked with him about some study and time management strategies and recommended that he meet with his teacher after school or during her planning period if he does not understand a concept. William's counselor also showed him how to set goals in order to better understand the content and get the work done. William decided to give it a try and eventually became comfortable with the struggle as he built his collection of success strategies.

If students rarely face challenge, then they rarely have an opportunity to bounce back from any kind of setback. That experience of bouncing back is an opportunity to practice and develop academic resiliency. Educators and students must conceptualize the idea that struggle means that they are learning.

Productive Struggle

We want students to be in the zone of learning that causes stretch or struggle. The challenge is that there is a fine line between productive struggle and frustration. Education authors Robyn Jackson and Claire Lambert described the difference between productive and destructive struggle (as cited in Allen, 2012).

Destructive struggle:

> Leads to frustration.
> Makes learning goals feel hazy and out of reach.
> Feels fruitless.
> Leaves students feeling abandoned.
> Creates a sense of inadequacy.

When a student (or teacher) is in a place of destructive struggle, he or she needs immediate intervention—the student may have run out of ideas/strategies for approaching the work. Sometimes his or her emotional regulation suffers as well.

Productive struggle:

> Leads to understanding.
> Makes learning goals feel attainable and effort seem worthwhile.
> Yields results.
> Leads students to feelings of empowerment and efficacy.
> Creates a sense of hope.

During productive struggle, students can wrestle with the task, try a variety of strategies, and eventually reach a solution.

Productive struggle is when students develop perseverance and academic resiliency. It is fine to provide some guidance to students during productive struggle—just don't overhelp. Ask a question that might trigger a strategy for them to try, or provide some scaffolding for support if needed. Guide students to ask questions that will trigger new thinking. Students need to learn about the importance of productive struggle. For teachers, the 2-minute video, "Teaching Habits That Promote Productive Struggle in Math" (https://www.youtube.com/watch?v=HAd8n5x0LxU), is worth a watch. Even though the video focuses on math, the habits described can be applied across content areas.

Reasoning games that build in difficulty are effective tools in building perseverance, resiliency, and applying strategies. In the video "Using Game-Based Learning in the Classroom to Develop Productive Struggle" (https://www.youtube.com/watch?v=0WlP8NNo4CU), MIND Research Institute (2016) presented game-based strategies that contribute to the development of student capacity for productive struggle. Games that progressively become more challenging are excellent tools in allowing students to get to the point of productive struggle. Some of the key points that are mentioned include:

> (Reasoning) games can engage students in effortful thinking.
> Games take a problem-based approach to learning.
> Games allow you to learn by doing, and therefore learn by failing.
> Games allow for informative feedback while students progress.
> Games allow for progressive growth. (They become more challenging.)

Many resources are available online that are specific to productive struggle in math; however, opportunities to struggle should not just be limited to math class. Teachers should provide opportunities across content areas for students to problem solve, wrestle with information, and think critically about content. Let students know that *struggle* is not a negative word—it just means they are giving their brains a great workout as they try to learn something new.

Discussion Questions

> Think of a time when you struggled through something before having success. How did you feel once you had success?

> What might be a first step in building a community that sees the value of productive struggle?

CHAPTER 5

Praise and Feedback

Building trusting relationships with your team and students should be an ongoing priority in your school. Positive relationships are the heart of building growth mindsets. Think about that for a minute. Aren't you more likely to respect feedback if you have a good rapport and respect for the person giving it? Creating good relationships allows for the development of resiliency and optimism in your team and students. School or central office leaders have conversations about learning with many stakeholders every day. The goal is to be aware of how we are communicating and if we are communicating in a way that cultivates growth and is focused on the process rather than the person.

How do we praise our students? Walking through almost any school, you will hear teachers praise student success, behaviors, and attitudes. Educators must be more aware of the way they praise students if they are journeying down the path of a growth mindset school culture. Carol Dweck and her colleagues presented sound evidence about the value of praising effort rather than outcome. Dweck (2006) discovered through her research that students who believe that intelligence is something you are born with and cannot change can be overly concerned with looking smart. Therefore, praise such as "You are so smart" could be detrimental for students who hold a fixed belief about intelligence. Saying "You are so smart" is the equivalent of saying "You are so tall"—what did a child have to do to be tall? Height is just a genetic trait that the child had no control over. Neither praise statement recognizes any action that the child has put forth. No effort is recognized. When adults praise what children "are," such as tall or smart, the children attribute their accomplishment to a fixed trait they were born with. When adults praise actions or tasks that children "do," the children attribute accomplishment to their own effort. Often moving toward growth mindset feedback is just a matter of adding on to the praise that is already stated. For example, if a teacher says, "You did a great job on that paper," she might add, "I can tell you worked very hard." Modifying or adding effort praise is all it takes to send a growth mindset message.

You might be thinking, "I like it when people say I am smart" or "I have seen kids beam with pride after I tell them they are smart," and you are correct; kids might feel good about themselves immediately after that compliment. What matters, however, is what happens later, when kids think, "She thinks I am smart, so I need to make sure I always look smart!" This kind of thinking can create risk-averse kids who will often avoid challenge so that they always have success.

The same fixed mindset thinking can happen to adults. We must be aware of the nonverbal messages that we send to our team as well as to our students. Folded arms, a stern face, a heavy sigh, or a roll of the eyes does not send a growth mindset message, no matter what words are coming from a person.

Schools should provide professional learning sessions for all adults in the office or school. These sessions should focus on ways to praise students (and each other) that value and promote growth. It is also important to put in place a support system that can provide feedback to teams. Peer coaching, an instructional coach, or school leadership can provide constructive, growth-focused feedback to all staff members. Adjusting feedback and praise is not as easy as it may sound—be purposeful with what is said to students and be patient with yourself as you work toward growth mindset praise and feedback. See Table 3 for some examples of ways to shift feedback statements with growth mindsets. I also highly recommend the 5-minute video, "Carol Dweck: A Study on Praise and Mindsets." It is a wonderful synthesis of Dweck's research about praise and should be shown in every central office department and every school! It can be found on the Train Ugly website: http:// trainugly.com/portfolio/praise-and-mindsets.

Deliberate instruction about the language you want to hear in school or district classrooms is time well spent. Let teachers and students know that the goal is to provide feedback and praise in a way that values their effort, strategies, critical thinking, struggle, willingness to take on more challenging work, and so forth. Explain that telling them they are smart, clever, creative, or brilliant doesn't give them feedback about what they have done; it only tells them who they are. It is important to communicate that both educators and students should speak to each other in this way.

We all need to strive for learning spaces in which members praise effort, struggle, and perseverance. Not only should we provide feedback and praise when educators and students select difficult tasks to conquer, but also when they try new strategies when learning a concept. Education leaders should work toward always praising the process not the person.

Sixth-grade teacher Ms. Montgomery was determined to introduce small-group math instruction this school year. Her plan was to preassess before each math unit and set up math groups based on the results.

TABLE 3

Shifting to Growth Mindset Feedback

Instead of . . .	Growth Mindset Feedback
You have five students below grade level in reading.	I can see that you have tried a lot of different strategies to reach these students. Tell me more about each student so that we might be able to figure out a way to support each one.
You should have spoken with Meghan's parents about the challenges she is having in class.	I can see that you tried to reach out to Meghan's parents many times and in different ways (persistence). Let's think about another way that we may be able to communicate with them.
Your small-group instruction is not working . . . too many students are off task.	I can see some improvement with your small-group instruction. Your students are not interrupting you when you are working with another group. Let's think about some ways we can help some of your students build their independent work skills.
When I walked around the room during your math class, I noticed that a lot of students were not understanding the concept.	I like the way you tried a variety of ways to teach that new math concept. What are some things that you might do to check for understanding along the way?
You are not entering your data into the student portal correctly.	I liked the effort you have put into entering student data into the portal. Let's work together and figure out why is it not displaying properly.

After the first few weeks of school, she explained the math group process to her students. After she analyzed the Unit One preassessment, she determined that she would have three instructional groups for math. Things were a little scattered the first day; she did not anticipate some of the overly energetic behaviors that were happening while she was working with the first group. She made a note to herself to set up some math anchor activities for students who finished early.

As luck would have it, the principal, Ms. O'Brien, walked into her class right in the middle of her first day of doing small groups. To Ms. O'Brien, the classroom looked chaotic with lots of students off task. Later that day, she e-mailed Ms. Montgomery and asked to speak to her after school. During the conversation, Ms. O'Brien said the following:

> "You are a great teacher."

> "You may not be able to manage three groups right away. Start with two."

The principal did not use process praise or feedback. She praised and provided feedback about the person: "You are . . ." and "You may not be able to . . ."

Instead, she could have used growth-focused praise:

> "It looks like you will be able to meet the needs of your math students with small-group instruction. I am glad you are taking a risk and trying this system."

> "What are some things that could be tried in order to have all students engaged in math when they are not in the teacher-led group?"

These are examples of providing feedback focused on the process.

The Power of the Word "Yet"

Additionally, one very important little word can make a world of difference for adults and students. That word is *yet*. *Yet* is an optimistic, hopeful word. It communicates the message that you are optimistic that someone will improve in time. Any learning environment, whether it is a classroom, a field, a court, in front of a piano, at the kitchen table, or a post-observation conference, should be a setting where both adults and students favor the word *yet*:

> "You are not quite there . . . *yet*. With more practice, you will be."
> "Your class reading data shows a lot of growth. Not every student is on level *yet*, but if you continue the strategies that you are using, they will be."
> "You haven't reached that particular student (or teacher) *yet*."

Keep the power of the word *yet* in mind as you embark on creating a growth mindset environment for your teachers and students. Challenge adults and children to talk themselves into a growth mindset when they find themselves thinking or saying things in a fixed mindset way. For example, if they think or say, "This is too hard for me," ask them for ideas about what they could think or say that would be more aligned with a growth mindset. Make an effort to practice giving growth mindset praise. It will take practice, perseverance, and a growth mindset!

Discussion Questions

> How might you respond to a student who is typically successful but does not have success on an assignment or assessment?
> What are some ways that you could implement growth mindset praise and feedback in your school or district?

CHAPTER 6

Setting the Stage for Professional Learning

Before getting started with professional learning sessions or a book study with your staff, spend some time alone or with your leadership team thinking about perceived and potential barriers as you build a growth mindset learning community. Doing this before you begin will help you consider different points of view as well as help you think through responses should they come up. (Sometimes I do this with school and office teams right after the first session in order to reduce behind-the-scenes chatter.) Figure 3 may help guide your thinking.

This may be a little tricky to grasp, but you actually have to apply growth mindset thinking in order to embrace the concepts of growth mindsets and fixed mindsets. Leaders must be constant learners, particularly with the rapid pace of change in education today. Leaders as learners can also model the importance of continuous learning for their teams. As education leaders,

Perceived and Potential Barriers Toward a Growth Mindset Environment

Possible Barrier	Proactive Plan to Address Barrier

FIGURE 3. Perceived and potential barriers toward a growth mindset environment. From *Ready-to-Use Resources for Mindsets in the Classroom: Everything Educators Need for Building Growth Mindset Learning Communities* (p. 15), by M. C. Ricci, 2015, Waco, TX: Prufrock Press. Copyright 2015 by Prufrock Press. Reprinted with permission.

we are all well aware of the importance of ongoing professional learning for ourselves and our teams. Learning Forward (2017) maintained the following beliefs:

1. Professional learning that improves educator effectiveness is fundamental to student learning.
2. All educators have an obligation to improve their practice.
3. More students achieve when educators assume collective responsibility for student learning.
4. Successful leaders create and sustain a culture of learning.
5. Effective school systems commit to continuous improvement for all adults and students. (para. 1)

In order to build a growth mindset learning environment, it is crucial to plan, facilitate, and follow up on ongoing professional learning sessions about mindsets. Our students are not the only learners who need to apply growth mindset thinking to their learning. School and district leaders must also adapt this thinking. One-and-done, "drive-through" professional learning sessions are not effective. The Every Student Succeeds Act (ESSA, 2015) defined professional development in the following way: "The term 'professional development' means activities that . . . are sustained (not stand-alone, 1-day, or short-term workshops), intensive, collaborative, job-embedded, data-driven, and classroom focused."

As leaders, we must commit to ongoing, multiyear learning centered around building a growth mindset learning environment. We must also be prepared for those educators on our team who will dig their heels in and not agree with the concept of malleable intelligence. I rarely speak to a group where I do not hear or see a version of one of the following fixed mindset comments:

> "Intelligence is genetic; I have had siblings in my class who had the same learning weaknesses."
> "There are some kids who will always be behind."
> "I guess this is another initiative that will go away in 6 months."
> "Smart, educated parents have smart kids."
> "My students live in poverty; there is no way they can work side by side with middle-class kids."

One of the most disturbing comments I heard from a central office leader was the following:

> "I have been here through four superintendents, and I will be here when this one leaves. There is no point in jumping aboard this initiative. It will be gone soon enough."

This comment also illustrates how important our own mindsets are as leaders. The good news is that because this statement was said out loud, we know where this leader's mindset really stands, and it is very likely that this fixed mindset thinking is applied to any new initiative. You may know others who feel the same way as this administrator, who just go through the motions, appear to be on board but do not have buy-in, and are just waiting until someone leaves.

Setting the Stage

When introducing the idea of becoming a growth mindset school or district to staff, I like to begin with something along the lines of:

> We are beginning a journey to becoming a growth mindset school (or district). It is not about learning a new set of standards, unpacking a new kit of materials, or writing detailed new lessons. It is about how we think about children and what we believe about intelligence. It is about looking at every child through a lens of potential and possibilities.

It is important to establish norms or ground rules for professional learning sessions. If time permits or if norms have not typically been used before, the participants should have input when establishing these norms. More details about establishing norms can be found here: https://learn ingforward.org/docs/tools-for-learning-schools/ tools8-99.pdf.

Here is a sample of norms that I have used in the past:
- › Honor time limits.
- › Be present.
- › Consider the possibilities.
- › Minimize distractions (e.g., cell phones, laptops, side bars).
- › Ask questions.
- › Have a growth mindset!

Where to Begin?

The first step is to get an idea of your team's knowledge base in regard to the concepts of fixed and growth mindsets. A reflection or preassessment are two options. It is also a good idea to try to capture what the team's beliefs are prior to any professional learning sessions so that you have a baseline that can be compared at a later date. In the past, I have asked educators to complete an online survey that includes scenarios of situations that may occur in the classroom (see Figure 4). Even though the situations described are aimed toward teachers, it is important to see how central office specialists, resource teachers, and administrators would respond because they support teachers. It is important to send out this survey (electronically through Google Surveys, SurveyMonkey, etc.) before the staff hears any discussion about mindsets in order to obtain true baseline data. You may want to send the same survey out again after at least a school year of transforming practices.

The next step is to plan your professional learning sessions. Ask yourself the following:

> Who will facilitate the professional learning sessions? The school or office administrator? A member of the school or office staff? The central office staff? An outside speaker or consultant?

> Are there funds available to hire an outside consultant/speaker?

> Should we partner with a neighboring school or district?

> Can we use a book study format? Will the book study be face-to-face, through an online discussion, or a hybrid?

> Will the calendar allow for at least quarterly professional learning sessions?

> What are some ways that we can monitor the application of what has been learned?

If you have a leadership team, these questions can be discussed together. Decide when the sessions will take place and make clear the expectations for attending. If possible, invite every adult who works in your office or school: the secretary, building service workers, cafeteria workers, etc. You may also want to consider inviting PTA (Parent Teacher Association) or

Educator's Mindset Reflection Tool

Please respond to the following scenarios according to what you personally would do if there were not outside influences or constraints (system or school expectations) on you. What do you feel is the BEST answer?

1. You have a child who is reading significantly below the rest of the class. Your English language arts class is about to start a text in which she has expressed significant interest. You plan to do the following:

   a. Give her a book on her reading level that deals with the same topic.

   b. Have her read the same book as everyone else—she's in this grade level and she has to read this.

   c. Have her read the book with a small group and provide frequent feedback.

   d. Have her read the abridged or graphic novel of the same text.

   Explain why you chose this response.

2. A student who consistently gets A's in other content areas fails one of your math tests. After determining the student is not having family or personal problems, what feedback do you give him?

   a. Math may not be your thing. Just try to pass!

   b. I'm here to help if you want it.

   c. You might want to change your strategy on how you're studying. You can do this!

   d. Nothing—the student will have to face the consequences of his actions.

   Explain why you chose this response.

FIGURE 4. Educator's mindset reflection tool. Adapted from *Ready-to-Use Resources for Mindsets in the Classroom: Everything Educators Need for Building Growth Mindset Learning Communities* (pp. 125–128), by M. C. Ricci, 2015, Waco, TX: Prufrock Press. Copyright 2015 by Prufrock Press. Adapted with permission.

3. Gifted education should:
   a. Identify students who are truly gifted and give them enrichment or acceleration opportunities.
   b. Provide differentiated enrichment and accelerated educational opportunities for all students.
   c. Identify students' interests and talents and provide development opportunities.
   d. Not exist—all students are gifted.

   Explain why you chose this response.

4. Special education should:
   a. Identify students with disabilities and provide remediation.
   b. Provide differentiated activities for multiple ways of learning for all students.
   c. Identify students who are struggling and provide supported education.
   d. Not exist—all students are special.

   Explain why you chose this response.

5. You have a student in your class who is normally well-behaved. This week, however, she does not stay on task and rarely finishes her work. You are currently studying current events, and you know that she is interested in science. How would you respond to her?
   a. Tell her that maybe current events isn't her "thing" and that next week, you will move on to a different topic.
   b. Give her work to do in science instead.
   c. Tell her that you appreciated the effort she put forth in the discussion.
   d. Ask her how she can see a connection between science and current events.

   Explain why you chose this response.

FIGURE 4. Continued.

6. You have a child who has been struggling significantly in your class. On today's test, he did very well. What do you say to him?
   a. Look how smart you are!
   b. I knew that you could do it!
   c. Looks like your hard work paid off!
   d. Nothing—he should be doing this well all the time.

   Explain why you chose this response.

7. You have an identified gifted child who is struggling with reading at grade level. You plan to put her in the following reading group:
   a. The low reading group, so that you can focus on her reading skills with similar students.
   b. A heterogeneous group, so that collaborative learning can be used.
   c. Self-selected groups, each focusing on a different text of interest.
   d. The high reading group, so that she can read challenging material.
   e. I don't group; all children get the same education based on the standards.

   Explain why you chose this response.

8. You have a child in special education who is reading just above grade level. You plan to put him in the following reading group:
   a. The low reading group, so that you don't pressure him and you can focus on his special needs.
   b. A heterogeneous group, so that collaborative learning can be used.
   c. Self-selected groups, each focusing on a different text of interest.
   d. The high reading group, so that he can read challenging material.
   e. I don't group; all children get the same education based on the standards.

   Explain why you chose this response.

FIGURE 4. Continued.

9. You have children with the following pre- and posttest scores:

Child	Pretest	Posttest
Noah	70%	85%
Jason	90%	95%
Ryan	10%	60%

Which child do you highlight as doing good work?

a. Noah
b. Jason
c. Ryan
d. None of them
e. All of them

Explain why you chose this response.

10. You have a child who is identified as gifted and is struggling in your math class. You plan to do the following:
    a. Teach him the math at his level, or collaborate with another teacher to help him at this level.
    b. Teach him the math that everyone else is working on—he's in this grade level and has to keep up.
    c. Have the rest of the class work on the regular assignment and show him more advanced math and explain how the skill you're working on is important for understanding the advanced math.
    d. Have the rest of the class work on the regular assignment and reteach him the original instruction.

    Explain why you chose this response.

Answer Key for #1–#10: A = Fixed, C = Growth

FIGURE 4. Continued.

PTO (Parent Teacher Organization) parent leaders. Sessions should be informative and interactive with time to reflect and plan. If some members of the staff already have a healthy knowledge of mindsets, then differentiate the learning or have them develop a tool or platform that will help your school or district move forward with growth mindset thinking.

Without a doubt, the question that I am asked the most by administrators is "Where should I start?" Table 4 offers an example of topics and tasks to use in the first two sessions.

There are many quality videos available that can be used during professional learning sessions. As professional learning sessions progress, leaders should walk through school buildings and look for signs of growth mindset thinking.

Discussion Questions

› Think about a way to approach professional learning in your school or district. How would you begin? Develop a draft plan.
› What do you anticipate as barriers? What are some ways that you might proactively address these perceived barriers?

TABLE 4
Professional Learning Session Topics and Exercises

	Topics	Exercise to Complete
Session 1 1 or 2 hours	What are mindsets, and why are they important? Show Khan Academy video, "You can Learn Anything" (https://www.khan academy.org/resources/parents-mentors-1/helping-your-child/v/you-can-learn-anything). Participants reflect on areas of their lives where they tend to apply fixed mindset thinking. Introduce the importance of growth-focused praise. Show video: "Carol Dweck: A Study on Praise and Mindsets" (https://www.youtube.com/watch?v=NWv1VdDeoRY).	Begin using growth mindset praise and feedback. Note the times when you slip up. Determine if there are any patterns when you use fixed mindset praise and feedback.
Session 2 1 or 2 hours	Discuss praise and feedback exercise and share challenges. Introduce the importance of deliberately cultivating perseverance and resiliency. Brainstorm ways to make perseverance and resiliency part of the school or district culture. Think about how you might monitor or collect data about how often students are exposed to discussions and learning experiences surrounding perseverance and resiliency.	Continue practicing growth mindset praise and feedback. Incorporate perseverance and resiliency into daily lessons.

CHAPTER 7

Procedures and Policies to Promote a Growth Mindset Environment

Whether we are aware of it or not, many of our school or district procedures, processes, and protocols do not complement a growth mindset culture. It doesn't matter how many growth mindset posters line the walls of schools or how well a team uses growth mindset praise and feedback. If your practices and procedures don't mirror the philosophical tenets of a growth mindset, you are not leading a growth mindset learning environment. Spend some time reflecting using the questions in Figure 5. After some reflection, collaborate and plan to revise some of these practices.

Some policies and practices can sabotage our goal for a growth mindset culture. In this chapter, we will focus on exploring some of those practices relating to grading, learning environment, behavior management, and hiring.

Are Your School or District Practices, Policies, Procedures, and Protocols Growth Mindset Friendly?

School or district leadership teams can use these questions when examining practices, policies, procedures, and protocols through the lens of a growth mindset. A growth mindset practice will have "yes" responses. If the practice leans toward a fixed mindset thinking, should the practice be eliminated or changed toward growth mindset thinking? Some questions to ask include:

> - Does the practice allow for equitable access—ongoing opportunities for students to access challenging instruction?
> - Does the practice value motivation, effort, interest, or student work ethic?
> - Is the practice responsive to the needs of students? (Or does it exist due to tradition or district/school history?)
> - Does it focus on process and/or growth rather than a cut-off score or grade?
> - Is the practice oriented to the positive?
> - Does it eliminate barriers and focus solely on the needs of individual students?
> - Does it address students' unmet academic needs?
> - What is the goal of the practice, policy, procedure, or protocol?
> - Should the practice be eliminated or can it be modified to support a growth mindset environment?
> - Is the practice set up to be flexible when a change is in the best interest of students?

FIGURE 5. Growth mindset friendly procedures and policies. Adapted from *Ready-to-Use Resources for Mindsets in the Classroom: Everything Educators Need for Building Growth Mindset Learning Communities* (p. 129), by M. C. Ricci, 2015, Waco, TX: Prufrock Press. Copyright 2015 by Prufrock Press. Adapted with permission.

Grades, Redos, and Retakes

Traditional grading is one of the areas that need to be examined in schools. Let's first consider grades on assignments done in school or for homework. Students need feedback, not a letter grade or percentage. With written or verbal feedback, they can be taught how to reflect on and learn from mistakes. Growth mindset thinking focuses on the process, the effort, the work ethic, and the application of strategies, not the outcome. For example, a student might work really hard on an assignment, put in the time and effort, and feel confident about his grade. However, if the student does not do well, he is likely to feel that all of the effort was wasted. The process and the end result (the grade) are not necessarily connected. Some students receive A's for putting forth very little effort, while others work hard for B's and C's. (Note that standards-based grading is more growth mindset friendly; either a child has mastered the standard or is not there yet.)

Think about some ways that you can use the act of grading an assignment to build on the concept of learning from failure. One approach that schools could adopt is this: Instead of putting an "X" next to an incorrect response (yes, this is still a practice in some schools—I have seen it with my own eyes!), just circle the response. Let students know that whenever they see a circle on a paper that they get back from the teacher, it means, "Look at this again" or "You don't quite get this yet." Then, provide the opportunity for them to reflect, revisit, and/or ask for clarification or reteaching of the item(s). If we really believe in the importance of learning from errors, we should allow students to redo assignments and retake assessments.

A growth mindset educator will work with students and guide or help them to approach the learning in a new way. We also need to provide time and space for practice and feedback. According to education author Rick Wormeli (2011):

> Many teachers reason that they are building moral fiber and preparing students for the working world by denying them the opportunity to redo assignments and assessments—or if they do allow retakes, by giving only partial credit for

redone assessments even when students have demonstrated full mastery of the content. These are the same teachers who set a deadline for submitting work and then give students who do not meet the deadline a zero, thinking that the devastating score will teach them responsibility.

In reality, these practices have the opposite effect: They retard student achievement and maturation. As hope wanes, resentment builds. Without hope—especially hope that teachers see the moral, competent, and responsible self inside them, waiting to shed its immature shell—students disengage from the school's mission and the adults who care for them. Our education enterprise is lost. (p. 22)

Additionally, if teachers do allow redos and retakes, they should not average scores together. Averaging grades does not communicate what a student understands. When you average a poor score on a test with a better score, you are actually representing what students previously did not understand, not what they presently understand. Don't most of us face a challenge the first time we try to do something new? Redos allow students to reflect and learn from errors and, most importantly, learn and master the material that is being taught.

The focus needs to shift to learning, not grades. I would argue that every assignment and assessment is actually a formative assessment. Think about that for a minute. Teachers don't grade formative assessments because they inform instruction. Information from formative assessments helps the teacher determine students' level of understanding and ways to help them get to their goals. Formative assessments are part of an ongoing process for students and teachers. Assignments in and out of school do the same thing; they tell us where a student is on the path to mastery. So, why do assignments and homework grades, especially those given when the learning is still new, "count" toward a student's final grade? Instead, useful feedback combined with a formative assessment can contribute to a growth mindset. Students and teachers (and parents) need to consistently value the learning, not the grade.

A growth-focused strategy that can be used when grading assignments or assessments is "My Favorite Mistakes." As teachers grade an assignment, test, or unit assessment, they can make note of some errors that they feel would provide an opportunity for students to better understand or internalize a concept. Either before or after passing back the reviewed assessments, teachers share their favorite mistakes with the class. Teachers can then use this opportunity to go over key concepts with the entire class or a small group. A video of seventh- and eighth-grade math teacher Leah Alcala implementing this strategy is a must-see. ("Highlighting Mistakes–A Grading Strategy" can be found at https://www.you tube.com/watch?v=BO2gndc4d9I.) In Leah's class, she does not even put a grade on the paper; students can check the grading portal for a grade if they wish. Rather than circling items, as I recommend, she highlights them (both ways are effective)—her focus is on the process, the learning, and the review, not the grade. This contributes to helping students frame mistakes or failures as a learning tool. As you watch, listen carefully as the students process the errors and to how Leah responds.

You might be thinking that, yes, this all sounds great, but your district has a grading policy that everyone must follow. Well, why not take another look at that policy and perhaps form a district grade and reporting committee to tackle a revised policy? In the meantime, if your teachers have no choice but to give grades based on school district policy, then teachers should keep the following points in mind.

Growth mindset teachers should:
> Use specific, written feedback rather than a percent or letter grade.
> Focus on what is understood, not what is wrong.

> › Grade for understanding of the content—no points off for a late assignment, unanswered questions, or if a student runs out of time. (In those cases, students are being graded for behavior, speed, and organization, not understanding.)
> › Not "count" a grade at the beginning of learning a new skill. (Every single assignment does not need a grade.)
> › Allow redos and retakes. (Drivers tests, the SAT, the ACT, and professional exams all allow retakes.)

Learning Environment

Is your school or district a fear-free zone? Do employees in your school or district feel comfortable sharing ideas, trying new things, providing honest feedback, and asking questions? School and district leaders must communicate through words and actions that ideas, feedback, and questions are not only welcomed, but also encouraged. A school or district should be continually spinning a wheel of improvement. This demands the input of stakeholders; the stakeholders must feel at ease when sharing ideas without being judged or frowned upon. We want our teams of educators to take intellectual risks—many do not come forth with ideas out of fear that their ideas will be dismissed or commented on in a negative way. This fear inhibits them from speaking up and encourages people-pleasing behaviors rather than problem solving. Intellectual risk-taking should be encouraged because of the potential to bring new information to the table, increase knowledge, and collaboratively solve problems. When a fear-free zone is established at the adult level, then we can expect the same thing to happen in our classrooms.

In addition to building a fear-free environment for the adults, we need to consider what is happening inside each classroom. A growth mindset classroom must be a safe place where students do not feel judged and are free to take intellectual risks. If it is not, then the fear-filled culture will sabotage your goal for a growth mindset learning community. A trusting, positive relationship between teacher and student is the heart of a secure learning environment. David Sousa and Carol Ann Tomlinson (2011) discussed the importance of empathy in the classroom as follows:

> Empathetic teachers ask themselves if they would want someone to say or do to them what they have just said or done to a student, colleague or parent. For instance, teachers sometimes try to motivate underperforming students by urging them to "try harder." Although the remark may be well intentioned, the teacher is assuming that the students are unwilling to expend the time and energy necessary to succeed. Consequently, students frequently construe this comment to be accusatory and judgmental. When students feel accused, they are less likely to be cooperative. (p. 20)

The learning environment *must* be a fear-free zone. Fear is such an intense emotion that it can shut down cognitive processes and force the brain to only focus on the source of the fear and what to do about it. The fear of making an error or experiencing failure is a big obstacle to learning. As mentioned earlier, some students will avoid experiences that may be too challenging due to fear of failure. A growth mindset teacher should discuss these fears with students and reassure them that they will not be judged if they make mistakes or fail. Teachers can also share their own stories of times when they were afraid to take a risk. Our environment helps to shape us, and a classroom learning environment does as well: "Just as adults are affected by their environments, students are encouraged or discouraged, energized or deflated, invited or alienated by classroom environments" (Sousa & Tomlinson, 2011, p. 31). Also important to note is that students may not feel supported in a learning environment where work is either too hard or too easy for them; thus, a differentiated, responsive classroom contributes to an intellectually safe learning environment.

Take a Look Around

Be aware of physical items in your school or district that might be unintentionally sending fixed mindset messages. Bulletin boards and displays should not be an array of A or perfect papers. Student work should be displayed, but think carefully about the message each assignment sends. For example, your school could highlight student growth by posting students' first drafts or first attempts at something alongside later attempts. Teachers can also display work that highlights the different strategies that students use to learn—perhaps examples of how two or three different students approached the same math problem in different ways. What about the names of those displays? Titles like "Top Dogs!" and "Hanging Out With Perfect Papers!" can send fixed mindset messages to kids. Instead a title like "Look How We Grow" can send a growth mindset message.

Look at the stickers or words that teachers use on students' papers or principals' comments on report cards. Do they say things like "Super Star!" or "Brilliant!"? Instead, try growth mindset messages like "Great effort!", "You're showing a lot of progress!", or "You don't quite get it *yet*." Take a look around your school or district: Is there anything else that might inadvertently sabotage your growth mindset space?

Think about events you have in your schools, such as awards programs and honor roll assemblies. They may elicit accolades for those children who reach a specific level of performance, but rarely consider that some "winners" put forth little effort to reach the mark and others put forth tremendous effort and are not recognized. An educator in Colorado explained that her school holds honor roll assemblies each quarter, and the same kids are always sitting in the back two rows—those who are never recognized.

She shared that these assemblies take place for two reasons: to motivate students who are not recognized (I don't think that is working because the same students always remain seated in the back) and because holding such assemblies is a tradition in the school that the parents expect. We need to look carefully at some of our school traditions.

What is the point of an honor roll assembly? If the point is to recognize good grades, I would argue that the "reward" could be the grade—if the student actually worked for it. Some students receive A's without putting forth a whole lot of effort (these students are likely underchallenged). If the point is to motivate others, then take note: Are the same students going unrecognized every time? Does an honor roll assembly really motivate others? An event such as this should shift its purpose to celebrate growth, perseverance, resiliency, and hard work rather than grades.

Classroom Management Policies

How do mindsets influence classroom management and behavior management systems? Take a closer look and reflect on the management system that is in place in your school or district through a growth mindset lens. Many behavior management systems that I see in schools rely on a public action that recognizes "inappropriate" behavior. For example, when a child's "card" is changed from green to yellow or yellow to red, it is noticed not only by the student, but also by the entire class. This approach is counter to growth mindset principles—it relies on shaming the student, not working on the skills needed to change the behavior. Instead, behavior management should focus on developing more appropriate behaviors. If children develop the skills needed to help them become responsible members of the school or classroom community, then behavior challenges will decrease. Approach behavior skills in the same way that you approach academics: Recognize the strengths that are demonstrated in students and provide them with the strategies and skills that they need in order to align to school guidelines. Believe in them, and if they are not quite there, be sure to include the word *yet* in your feedback so that they know you believe that they will improve. Build an optimistic relationship with students—this is more important than the right set of rules.

> Sophia, a fifth-grade student, was very excited about a learning experience that was being presented in class. In Sophia's excitement, she forgot that the teacher said that students had to stay in their seats. She jumped out of her seat and excitedly shared something that she knew about the topic. Immediately, Sophia's teacher asked her to go over to the clip chart hanging in the class and move her behavior clip to a lower level.
>
> What just happened here? Sophia was excited about what they were learning, but then she was publicly shamed for getting a little too excited about the teaching that was taking place.

When I have asked teachers about behavior systems like this one, more times than not, they explain that the system is in place to "control" behavior. What message does that send? Our goal should not be to control, but instead to let kids know that we are confident that they can solve problems and make appropriate choices about behavior. Systems that try to control students also do not allow for reflection. When students make choices that do not conform to school or classroom rules, they must be provided an opportunity to think about and reflect on the decision that they made and the consequences of that decision. Some students also need to work on the skills required to self-regulate, but they may not know what those skills are yet. Online resources and many books can be consulted for guidance for those students who need additional support with self-regulation.

Additionally, in order to apply growth mindset thinking toward inappropriate actions that are taking place, educators should take time to try to figure out why these students are acting out. Doing so may help them figure out if there is an underlying issue, and if so, what kinds of strategies the child might need. Educators who apply growth mindset thinking toward student behavior mirror an instructional approach—that is, students need to learn both academic and behavioral skills that they have not yet developed.

Educators who apply fixed mindset thinking are more likely to attribute behaviors to who the child is, and may have difficulty separating the behavior from the child. Let students know that we all make behavior mistakes, but the trick is to stop, think about the mistake (reflect), and move on or remedy the mistake that was made if possible. A good place to begin is to identify just one behavior pattern you have observed in your school (e.g., hitting, cheating, disrupting class, etc.). Collaborate as a staff on a plan to teach the skills needed to address this area.

Not sure where to begin? Ask yourself these questions:

> Who are the frequent visitors to the principal's office (or assistant principal's office, dean's office, etc.)?
> What was each student's "offense"?
> Do you, as an administrator, notice a pattern? What is the most prevalent behavior that you see?

That behavior is where you should consider beginning to teach the skills needed to change the behavior.

Vince Naccarato, Principal of Reno Valley Middle School, USD 309 Nickerson South Hutchinson, outside of Hutchinson, KS, saw positive changes in his seventh- and eighth-grade students after he and his team began to focus on nurturing a growth mindset community. Reno Valley's staff embraced the growth mindset concept, and it changed how the staff communicated with students, especially in regard to learning from mistakes. The school adopted a behavior management system inspired by the Responsibility-Centered Discipline model by Larry Thompson (AccuTrain Corporation, 2018). The leadership team at Reno Valley Middle School created "Pillars of Belief" that are consistently discussed with students. You can find a poster of these pillars in every classroom (see Figure 6). The team also set up an "Advisory Class" that meets twice a week to further cultivate students' skills in perseverance and resiliency. These skills are practiced daily as students are exposed to new content in all classes. What I find interesting about the pillars they established is that each of the statements can be applied to both academics and behavior. The following are the school norms with my behavior interpretation under each in italics.

At Reno Valley Middle School, we will develop a growth mindset:

> › By working to correct the problem and learn from it when I make a mistake.
>
>   *Did I make a bad behavior choice? What can I learn from it, and how can I change things to lessen the chance of a repeat?*

> › By being persistent in my efforts when I start to struggle.
>
>   *If I find myself beginning to struggle with behavior expectations, I need to make sure that I deliberately practice appropriate actions.*

> › By recognizing that success takes practice and hard work.
>
>   *In order to consistently follow behavior guidelines, I must practice and be dedicated to working toward success.*

Reno Valley also recognizes students who show the most growth in math, as well as those students who demonstrate grit and persistence. This kind of recognition influences student behavior in a positive way. Reno Valley's math teacher, Trissa McCabe, reflected,

> In this day and age where speed and immediacy is everything, to help promote the growth mindset in my classroom I have found myself saying, "I'm going to give you a little more think time to

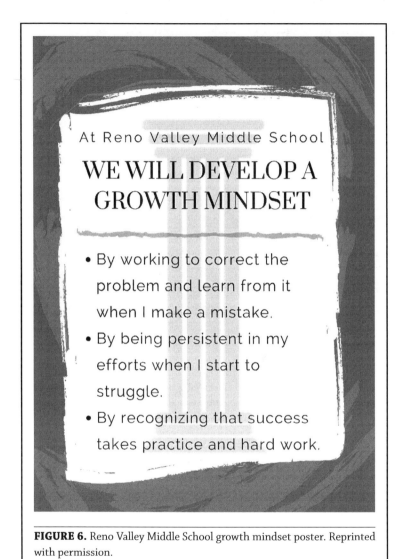

FIGURE 6. Reno Valley Middle School growth mindset poster. Reprinted with permission.

work through it." It's okay to stop and think. In fact, that's what our businesses are asking for, students that can think!

McCabe speaks for many of the teachers at Reno Valley Middle School who are seeing a difference in kids every day due to the changes that they have made as a staff.

Hiring

How can we attract new team members to our office and schools whose educational philosophies jive with growth mindset principles? Frederick County Public Schools in Maryland started this search in the Human Resources department. Among their recruitment literature, they communicate their commitment to growth mindsets (see Figure 7).

What kind of interview questions and scenarios could you present to a candidate for employment that would really underscore core beliefs about mindsets? Here are some interview questions for discerning mindsets when hiring principals, instructional coaches, central office resource teachers, or specialists:

> - How would you approach a teacher who is reluctant to change?
> - Have you ever experienced a leadership do-over? (You made a mistake, let people know, and then approached the situation in a different way.)
> - Was there ever a time when you didn't meet a goal? What did you do about it?
> - Share a time in your life when you stepped out of your comfort zone to accomplish something difficult.
> - Who is most responsible for student learning? Why?
> - A parent approaches you with concerns about how students are grouped by ability. How would you address his or her concerns?
> - A principal at an underperforming school does not appear to be doing much to increase achievement. How might you work with him or her?
> - A staff member communicates that the new teacher on the team is not collaborating or being an active partici-

> FCPS is proud to be a growth mindset school system, with a strong belief in risk-taking and continuous growth!
>
> We are:
> - Purposely infusing growth mindset in instruction at all levels.
> - Providing staff with a developed FCPS Growth Mindset School Culture Framework to guide professional learning and staff growth.
> - Developing competencies in Mind Brain Education and neuroplasticity.
> - Providing growth-focused feedback and praise.
> - Ensuring equitable access for students to advanced learning opportunities.
> - Developing psychosocial skills like perseverance, resilience, and grit.
> - Providing professional learning that focuses on development of growth mindsets in students and staff at all levels of the system.
>
> ---
>
> **FIGURE 7.** Frederick County Public Schools HR recruitment brochure.
>
> This work is licensed under a Creative Commons Attribution-NonCommercial-ShareAlike 4.0 International License (https://creativecommons.org/licenses/by-nc-sa/4.0/). Reprinted here with permission of the author.

pant in data chats. She leaves meetings early by saying that she needs time to prepare for her class. As a principal, what would you do?

Try questions like these for teachers and paraeducators:
- Do you feel that all students can succeed? Explain why.
- What are some ways that you praise and provide feedback to your students?
- How might you approach a student with low motivation?
- How would you respond to a child who says, "I can't"?
- What strategies would you use to help students reach goals?
- Tell me about your grading policies.
- What would you do to help a struggling learner?
- How do you foster student growth in your classroom?

> › Do you feel that there is a correlation between student grades and success?
> › How would you address a student who has historically received "failing" grades on his or her report card?

The Human Resources office may be able to develop scenarios customized for your district. The scenarios that are developed would require a candidate to respond in a way that would reveal fixed or growth-oriented thinking.

Discussion Questions

> › Think about special events that occur in your school or district. Do these events communicate fixed or growth mindset messages?
> › What are some things that you can do to encourage intellectual risk-taking with your team?
> › Think about some authentic scenarios that could be used when interviewing a potential new team member.

CHAPTER 8

Parent and Community Involvement

Building a growth mindset community needs to extend outside the schoolhouse and into the community. Parents, coaches, scout leaders, afterschool clubs, and sports facilitators should all complement the work that is going on in school. We want parents, coaches, and tutors to use the same language and be on the same page as district and school staff. Educators want parents to understand that mistakes and failure are part of the learning process and struggle is not a bad thing. Schools can try a variety of experiences to get parents involved: book clubs, growth mindset game nights, principal coffees, and professional learning workshops for parents. If possible, involve parents in planning your growth mindset school community. Invite a few parent representatives to be part of a school or district mindset committee, or invite them to a leadership team meeting when plans are being made. Encouraging parents to share their input and take part in the planning not only helps them understand the content more deeply, but also gives them some ownership in the process and forms a partnership with a common goal. In turn, they will talk to other parents at the bus stop, at the sports field, at church, and at neighborhood gatherings.

Districts can also offer growth mindset as part of the training for leaders of afterschool activities and sports. Jennifer Beaverson, PTA president of Hammond Elementary School in Howard County, MD, shared:

> My son's school has embraced Growth Mindset and weaves lessons into the curriculum to expose the students to the concepts. As a result of the school's commitment to Growth Mindset concepts, you will find parents at the park or at school events, having conversations about the power of 'yet' and resiliency. It has provided parents with a valuable common language to describe the struggles kids face and the tools they possess to combat the "I can'ts." (personal communication, April, 24, 2018)

This chapter provides some resources that will help administrators reach out and communicate with the greater parent community. Schools with diverse student populations must keep in mind that these resources should be translated into other languages, and parent meetings/workshops must be made accessible to the majority of your parent community. Plan a growth mindset parent night, making it as accessible as possible for your community to attend. Consider providing free babysitting (high school students who need community service hours work well) and/or provide pizza or dessert/coffee. Create a welcoming environment so that the event will attract a great number of parents and guardians.

Introduce growth mindset step-by-step. After a growth mindset parent night, or a brief introduction to fixed and growth mindsets during a back-to-school night or before a PTA meeting, send out ideas and reminders to revisit or expand on the ideas presented face-to-face. Figure 8 can be used to do just that. This resource is broken down into seven sections, each focusing on a different goal toward helping parents develop a growth mindset home environment. Schools should send each part out separately so that parents can focus on changes a little at a time. If too much information is given at once, it may decrease the chance that the resource will be read in its entirety. (I'll admit: I am quite guilty of just skimming extended notices that my kids bring home or that are sent out electronically.)

Breaking the ideas down into small steps will also increase the chance that families will participate because the tasks become more doable and not so overwhelming. This approach is particularly helpful for families whose practice is more "fixed" than "growth." These steps can be sent home (on paper or electronically) weekly, every few weeks, or monthly. It would also be interesting to create an online space (blog, Facebook group, etc.) where parents can share their ideas, struggles, and questions as they embrace growth mindset principles. Schools and districts can also add more specific ideas related to their community, such as a local rock-climbing wall or a library reading program that might require perseverance from the children.

One of the most effective ways that I have found to guide parents deep into the understanding of mindsets is by having a book club using *Mindsets for Parents: Strategies to Encourage Growth Mindsets in Kids* (Ricci & Lee, 2016). Discussion questions are included in the book, so your team does not have to generate them or participate in the parent group. I have visited several of these parent groups, and the questions and discussion that take place are energizing. I also happen to know that one or both authors will visit local (Washington, DC, Maryland, and Virginia) groups or Skype with faraway groups when their schedules permit. A Spanish translation of the book is currently in the works as well. When it is ready, it will be announced via social media on Twitter (@MaryCayR) and Facebook (https://www.facebook.com/MindsetsForParents).

Ideas for Creating a Growth Mindset Environment at Home

Ideas for Creating a Growth Mindset Environment at Home Part 1:

Parents Work Toward a Growth Mindset for Themselves

› We can't expect our children to have a growth mindset if we don't have one ourselves. Recognize fixed mindset thinking in yourself and talk yourself into a growth mindset. This can also be done out loud so that your child can hear how you are changing your mindset. For example, you might catch yourself saying, "I can't figure out how to fill out this document." Then quickly rephrase it to add, "I think I need to check on the website or call the bank so I can ask some questions. Then I am sure I will be able to fill it out accurately."

› Be aware of your own fixed mindset statements such as "I am a terrible cook," "I was never good at math either," or "I wish I could play the piano like you do." (You can, with practice and perseverance!)

› Be aware of blaming genetics for anything—both positive and negative.

› Be careful about comparing your kids to their siblings or other kids.

› We want our children to enjoy the process of learning—not just be successful. Model this concept at home. For example, after a less than desirable outcome trying to bake something challenging, you might say "I really learned a lot making those cookies" rather than "Ugghh, what a waste of time. That was an epic fail. I will never try that recipe again."

FIGURE 8. Ideas for creating a growth mindset environment. From *Ready-to-Use Resources for Mindsets in the Classroom: Everything Educators Need for Building Growth Mindset Learning Communities* (pp. 67–70), by M. C. Ricci, 2015, Waco, TX: Prufrock Press. Copyright 2015 by Prufrock Press. Reprinted with permission.

Ideas for Creating a Growth Mindset Environment at Home Part 2:

Using Growth Mindset Praise and Feedback

> Praise what your child does, not who he or she is. Instead of saying, "You are so smart/clever/brilliant," say "I can see you really worked hard/put forth effort/tried hard." Praise perseverance and resiliency when you see your child struggle or face challenge. Avoid praising grades. Focus on praising work ethic and effort—not achievement.

> Adopt the word "yet" into your vocabulary. If your child proclaims that he doesn't understand something, can't dribble a basketball, or can't play a song on his guitar, remind him that he can't "yet" but with hard work he will have success.

> Avoid comparing your child's success with that of siblings or friends—achievement is not a competition. There is enough success for everyone.

Ideas for Creating a Growth Mindset Environment at Home Part 3:

Redirecting Fixed Mindset Thinking

> Redirect your child's fixed mindset statements. If you hear your child say "I am no good in math" or "I just can't understand Shakespeare," point out the fixed mindset thinking and direct her to a growth mindset place. Remind her that she may not understand yet, but will by asking questions, finding new strategies, setting small goals, and working hard. Two examples of how to redirect such statements are included below.

If Your Child Says	Then You Might Say
"I am no good in math."	"You may not understand this yet, so let's practice some more."
"I don't need to study; I always do well on math assessments."	"Studying can help prime the brain for further growth. Maybe you should let your teacher know that these assessments don't require much practice for you and that you are willing to take on more challenge."

FIGURE 8. Continued.

Ideas for Creating a Growth Mindset Environment at Home Part 4:

Struggle

> Help your child become curious about errors or lack of success. Remind your child that failure is important on the way to success. Model this!
> Show your child the Michael Jordan *Failure* commercial (available at https://www.youtube.com/watch?v=45mMioJ5szc and only 30 seconds long). Talk to your child about what the last line of the video means.
> Provide some puzzles and games that may create a little struggle for your child. Work together and discuss why struggle shows that you are learning and that you can build resiliency.
> Model and encourage resiliency—the ability to bounce back from errors and failures.

Ideas for Creating a Growth Mindset Environment at Home Part 5:

Flexibility and Optimism

> Model flexibility. Communicate that change is an important part of living life. Model this by taking a flexible mentality when things don't go as planned. Don't let frustrating situations get the best of you—make your children aware of your ability to adapt due to a change in plans. Praise your children for their flexibility and adaptability when plans change or success is not met.
> Model optimism. Adopt a "glass half full" mentality in your home. A person with "hope" believes there can be a positive side to most situations.
> Play a game with your kids: For every time something happens that is perceived as "bad," try to find the good in every situation. This game can get a little silly but it gets a message of positivity across. For example, when a glass is accidentally broken, a possible response might be, "Now we have more room on our shelf!"

FIGURE 8. Continued.

Ideas for Creating a Growth Mindset Environment at Home Part 6:

Learning and the Brain

> Talk about neural networking. Ask your child what he or she has learned in school about the brain.
> Whenever you hear your child say "I give up" or "I just don't get this," remind your child to visualize neurons connecting every time he learns something new. Encourage your child to work hard and practice new skills and concepts so that he can develop strong neural connections in his brain.
> Share with your child some things that you have not yet mastered and your plan for practicing and building stronger connections in your brain.

Ideas for Creating a Growth Mindset Environment at Home Part 7:

Developing Important Psychosocial Skills

> A child's innate ability contributes to only about 25% of achievement. The other 75% are psychosocial skills that must be deliberately developed. The important skills we can help our children develop include:
>   • perseverance,
>   • self-confidence,
>   • resiliency,
>   • coping skills for disappointment and failure, and
>   • the ability to handle constructive feedback.

> Choose books to read with younger students that highlight characters that demonstrate these skills. Discuss these with your child.
> When watching TV or a movie with your kids, talk about a character's strength or lack of perseverance or resiliency. Ask your children how the situation or story would be different if the person did or did not have this skill.
> Name the psychosocial skills words and use phrases that represent these around the house. For example, you might say, "My supervisor gave me some constructive feedback about how I can do my job better. I am grateful for that because she gave me some new things to try" or "I was watching you (climb that tree, play that video game, figure out the new cell phone, etc.) today. You really showed determination and perseverance!"

FIGURE 8. Continued.

Discussion Questions

> Do you anticipate any pushback from parents about the principles of a growth mindset learning environment? If so, what would they be concerned about, and how might you address these concerns?

> Think about ways that your school or district communicates with parents. How can your already established communication methods be used to impart important growth mindset reminders?

CHAPTER 9

Curriculum and Instruction

This chapter will focus on ways to embed growth mindset principles into content area curriculum and instruction. Ideas will be presented for major content areas; however, I encourage you to adapt and develop ideas for all areas. Perhaps you are a supervisor of English language learners at the central office. What are some ways that you can develop learning experiences for English language learners so that the students can build academic resiliency? Are you a director of transportation or food services? Is there a way that you can provide an overview of growth mindset praise and feedback to your bus drivers and cafeteria workers so that they will speak to students in a way that acknowledges effort? Whether or not curriculum and instruction are developed at the central office or at a local school, think about ways that growth mindset principles can be embedded, and not "add-ons" to an already overcrowded curriculum. Here are a few ideas and resources.

English Language Arts

One of the most effective ways to encourage growth mindset thinking is through literature. Take a look at the books and anthologies in your curriculum that are used at each grade level. For each grade level, identify the text pieces that could be used to demonstrate growth and/or fixed mindset thinking—tenacity, grit, resiliency, persistence, perseverance, work ethic, optimism, goal setting, etc. Develop a few sample questions that teachers could ask that would ignite a thoughtful discussion.

If you have the budget for additional books or library purchases, *Ready-to-Use Resources for Mindsets in the Classroom* (Ricci, 2015) provides a list of 50 picture books and 25 extended texts along with the authors' names, recommended grade levels (although I am a fan of using picture books at every level), date published, and whether each character or story demonstrates a fixed mindset, growth mindset, or both. Also included is a column that refers to any evidence from the story that supports the mindset, as well as some growth mindset discussion questions.

Since that list was published, I have found some more wonderful books to consider (see Figure 9).

An effective book for teaching and conceptualizing mindsets for students in grades 3–7 is *Nothing You Can't Do!: The Secret Power of Growth Mindsets* (Ricci, 2018), which is actually a partner book with this one, *Mindsets in the Classroom* (Ricci, 2017), and *Mindsets for Parents* (Ricci & Lee, 2016). *Nothing You Can't Do!* can be used with any class or group learning about mindsets, including counseling groups, study skills classes, and middle school transition courses. It could also be used as a nonfiction text in an ELA course or as a recommended summer reading book.

Additionally, during a biography unit, curriculum writers can recommend biographies of people who demonstrated a growth mindset. Students can be encouraged to choose to read about people who model perseverance, resiliency, optimism, and work ethic. Some of those people include: Susan B. Anthony, Cesar

Title of Book	Author
Picture Books	
Ada Twist, Scientist	Andrea Beaty
Be Positive! A Book About Optimism	Cheri J. Meiners
The Bear and the Piano	David Litchfield
The Book of Mistakes	Corinna Luyken
Dream Something Big: The Story of the Watts Towers	Dianna Hutts Aston
Drum Dream Girl: How One Girl's Courage Changed Music	Margarita Engle
Emmanuel's Dream: The True Story of Emmanuel Ofosu Yeboah	Laurie Ann Thompson
Hana Hashimoto, Sixth Violin	Chieri Uegaki
I Won't Quit	Danny McGill
Jabari Jumps	Gaia Cornwall
Not Yet	Lisa Cox and Lori Hockema
One Word From Sophia	Jim Averbeck
Puppy Mind	Andrew Jordan Nance
Shark Lady: The True Story of How Eugenie Clark Became the Ocean's Most Fearless Scientist	Jess Keating
She Persisted: 13 American Women Who Changed the World	Chelsea Clinton
Sky Pig	Jan L. Coates
The Thing Lou Couldn't Do	Ashley Spires
When Sophie Thinks She Can't	Molly Bang
Extended Texts	
Amina's Voice	Hena Khan
Fish in a Tree	Lynda Mullaly Hunt
Nothing You Can't Do!: The Secret Power of Growth Mindsets	Mary Cay Ricci

FIGURE 9. Books that promote growth mindsets.

Chavez, Misty Copeland, Walt Disney, Albert Einstein, Milton Hershey, Steve Jobs, Nelson Mandela, Sonia Sotomayor, Harriet Tubman, and Wilma Rudolph.

Teachers can also place emphasis on building a conceptual understanding of the following words during vocabulary study: *tenacity, grit, perseverance, persistence, stick-to-itiveness, determination, stamina, endurance, diligence, drive,* and *resiliency.*

Science

Chances are that almost every scientist and researcher that your students learn about demonstrated a growth mindset. Persistence and tenacity are important when creating experiments and doing research. Make sure that these attributes, along with the importance of learning from failure, are embedded into your science curriculum. Additionally, science is the perfect place to dive deeper into those neuroscience lessons to teach kids about the brain—specifically neural connections. (For more information on neuroscience and mindsets, see Appendix C.) During a health class, be sure to include discussion surrounding food and sleep habits that promote healthy brains.

A Makerspace can also be an ideal environment for learning about mindsets. Makerspaces are spaces where innovation and problem solving flourish; students can explore, innovate, persevere, and learn from struggle and failure. Makerspaces can be small areas of a larger room (e.g., a corner of the media center, the stage in an all-purpose room, a section of the science lab) or a rolling cart with maker materials. With the current emphasis on STEAM education, creative problem solving, and innovation, consider working Makerspaces into your curriculum framework. As a central office supervisor in a large system, I worked collaboratively with the library/media office as well as arts integration to build a framework for the exploration that would occur in these spaces. There was a focus on risk-taking and embracing errors and failures as students explored the materials that focused on building the concept of circuits.

If this is new ground for your school or district, then take a small step. Perhaps offer an afterschool enrichment program to get started. Reflect and learn from the experience, and then embed the experience into the school day. Innovation occurs when we have the courage and comfort to make mistakes and learn from them; this applies to students as well as the adults who develop programs for them.

Social Studies

Take a look at your social studies curriculum and highlight historians who have demonstrated a growth mindset. Identify communities around the world that have had to rebuild due to war, weather, or financial challenges.

Find texts with authentic stories of failure. For example, *National Geographic* has a great article for students in grades 7–12 that looks at famous explorers and how failure plays a part in exploration. "Failure Is an Option" by Hannah Bloch (2013) can be found at https://www.nationalgeographic.com/magazine/ 2013/09/famous-failures (this is also a nice piece of text to read in conjunction with the novel *Shackleton's Stowaway* by Victoria McKernan). Lots of discussion points are evident in this article, including the following quote:

> "I learned how *not* to climb the first four times I tried to summit Everest," says alpinist Pete Athans, who's reached the world's highest peak seven times. "Failure gives you a chance to refine your approach. You're taking risks more and more intelligently." (para. 4)

Identify other texts that give real accounts of the value of failure so that students can see how failure can have a positive impact in many aspects of life.

Mathematics

My first recommendation is to read the book *Mathematical Mindsets* by Jo Boaler (2016). This book will help lay the groundwork for developing growth mindset friendly instructional experiences for your students. In the article "Jo Boaler Wants Everyone to Love Math," Sam Scott (2018) explained:

> As a researcher, teacher and evangelist, Boaler is a leading voice for a wholly different pedagogy where speed is out, depth is in, and the journey to an answer can be as important as the destination. It's an approach where sense-making matters more than memorization and retaining "math facts" matters less than understanding how such facts interconnect. (para. 6)

Additionally, build a guidance document that complements your curriculum and that continually revisits the importance of productive struggle. Some good resources include:

> › "Promoting Productive Struggle in Math" by Michael Giardi: https://www.edutopia.org/article/promoting-productive-struggle-math

> › "8 Teaching Habits that Block Productive Struggle in Math Students" by Heera Kang: https://blog.mindresearch.org/blog/productive-struggle-in-math

> › "Teaching Habits that Promote Productive Struggle in Math" by MIND Research Institute: https://www.youtube.com/watch?v=HAd8n5x0LxU

The Arts

Almost every time I ask a group of people, "In what areas of your life do you find yourself having a fixed mindset?" at least one person says, "I cannot draw" or "I am a terrible singer." The arts seem to be an area where fixed mindset thinking is prevalent. Leaders who influence curriculum and instruction in the arts should build in time early in the year to talk about the malleability of the brain. This lets students know that, with deliberate practice, everyone can show growth in music, visual arts, and performance arts.

Educators can also identify artists who overcame challenges throughout their lives—perhaps a few painters who were never recognized for their art, yet continued to paint what are now considered masterpieces. The article "10 Incredible Artists Unappreciated in Their Time" (https://www. onlineuniversities.com/blog/2010/11/10-incredible-artists-unappreciated-in-their-time) has a good list of painters, musicians, and writers.

Physical Education (PE)

The physical education teacher at Howard County Maryland Elementary, Suzy Serpico, communicates growth mindset messages to her students. She shared that:

> Learning about Growth Mindset has helped me both personally and professionally. Reflecting on 20 years as a competitive athlete, I realize that I owe a great deal of my success to a Growth Mindset. Implementing Growth Mindset in my elementary Physical Education instruction has been successful and rewarding. Many children compare their athletic skills to others and feel they don't measure up. Educating them on the skills

and vocabulary of Growth Mindset has increased their confidence, their determination, their perseverance, and often, their performance. I wholeheartedly endorse the use of Growth Mindset in Physical Education programs. (personal communication, April 24, 2018)

Reflection Across All Areas

Regardless of the content area or department, guidance documents can be developed that can highlight areas where a growth mindset can be emphasized. These documents could include reminders to teachers about the importance of reflection when students are learning.

Educator Jackie Gerstein (2016) identified several reflective practices to consider. She recommended the following for reflection during instruction:

> › Structure lesson plans to support reflective thinking.
> › Provide lesson components that prompt inquiry and curiosity.
> › Provide resources and hands-on tasks that prompt exploration.
> › Provide reflective thinking opportunities that prompt students to think about what they have done, what they have learned, and what they still need to do.

Although all of these practices are important, the last bullet really complements growth mindset thinking. Think about your school or district—do you observe any of these reflective practices on a daily basis?

Additionally, education advocate and writer Rusul Alrubail (2015) proposed the following benefits of reflection:

> › **Significance:** It allows students to see the importance of their own learning process.

> › **Process Recognition:** Students can identify what they did well, what they failed at, what they need to change.
> › **Solutions/Strategies:** Provides students an opportunity to come up with solutions and strategies to improve on their learning.
> › **Motivation:** Reflection provides students with motivation to learn and enjoy the process of learning. This motivation comes from them reflecting on their thoughts, feelings and emotions.
> › **Analysis:** The most important benefit of reflection in the classroom is for students to be able to know *why* they needed to learn these concepts, theories, and ideas.
> › **Learning Won't Be Content Driven:** It's important for students to know "how" to learn and how to continue to be learners. Memorizing content will not help students become critical thinkers. Critical thinking stems from pausing, reflecting, and knowing "how" and "why" learning should be happening at that moment. (para. 2)

These are all integral components of a growth mindset learning environment. What are some ways that you can increase these behaviors in your school or district?

Formative Assessment

Harman School principal Sarah Patterson of Oakwood City School District in Ohio looks for evidence of growth mindset during her daily walkthroughs. In addition to noting all of the perseverance praise she hears, she shared that one of her favorite observations were the exit slips from the school counselor's grade 4 lesson about growth mindset. These exit slips (see Figure 10) served as a formative assessment to help determine how well students understood the concepts of mindsets and neuroplasticity.

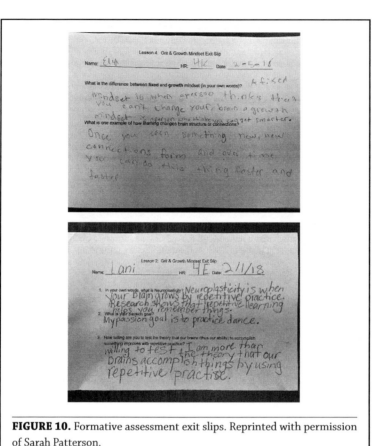

FIGURE 10. Formative assessment exit slips. Reprinted with permission of Sarah Patterson.

Here are a few more ideas for implementing formative assessment in your curriculum and instruction:

> **Use questions for students to respond to orally.** During the course of instruction or on the way out of the door (in middle school and high school), ask students to respond to various questions regarding the learning that occurred during class. Make note of those students who have misunderstandings or have not yet grasped the learning.

> **Use questions for students to respond to in writing.** Provide students with a few questions that will help them reflect on their understanding of the concept.

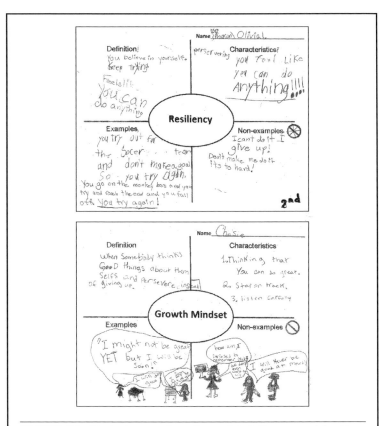

FIGURE 11. Student examples of completed Frayer models. From *Ready-to-Use Resources for Mindsets in the Classroom: Everything Educators Need for Building Growth Mindset Learning Communities* (p. 30), by M. C. Ricci, 2015, Waco, TX: Prufrock Press. Copyright 2015 by Prufrock Press. Reprinted with permission.

> › **Use a 3-2-1.** A 3-2-1 can be customized depending on the content and grade level. A generic form of a 3-2-1 might provide students an opportunity to express orally or in writing the following: 3 Things I Learned Today, 2 Things I Have Questions About, 1 Thing That I Want to Learn More About.
>
> › **Use a Frayer Model.** Ask students to provide examples, nonexamples, list characteristics, and create a visual representation of a concept (see Figure 11).

Differentiated, Responsive Instruction

The mindset of a teacher or administrator contributes greatly to his or her responsiveness to the needs of students. If an educator views a child through a deficit lens, then that child will not be given opportunities to grow unless she is in a responsive school and classroom. Deficit thinking is a practice of making assumptions about a child's ability based on perceived deficits or because of race, low-income status, English language acquisition, or a variety of other factors. Educators who value differentiated instruction need to be very aware of the beliefs they hold deep within themselves regarding student intelligence. I would argue that it is not possible to plan and facilitate an effective, differentiated, responsive classroom if an educator does not really possess the belief that intelligence can develop.

As a curriculum developer, take a look at what is available at each grade level. Are preassessments a part of your curriculum documents? Do pathways exist for students who already demonstrate understanding?

Discussion Questions

> As an education leader who is responsible for curriculum and instruction, what are some ways that you can thread growth mindset principles across all aspects of your district?

> What are some ways that you could update your present curriculum to include explicit lessons about fixed and growth mindsets?

CHAPTER 10

A Growth Mindset School District

Frederick County Public Schools (FCPS) is a school system in Maryland that serves approximately 42,000 students. (It is considered a midsized district in Maryland, but is a large district in the context of most of the U.S.) Superintendent Dr. Theresa Alban has made sure that growth mindset thinking is front and center throughout the school system. Dr. Alban is an innovative superintendent and shared with me the three areas of focus that FCPS has been working toward over several years:

1. high-quality instruction,
2. cultural proficiency, and
3. growth mindset.

For several years the district has been providing professional learning and infusing the concept of growth mindset across many aspects of the district (see Figure 7, p. 75). The Advanced

Academics Supervisor and coauthor of *Mindsets for Parents*, Margaret (Meg) Lee, has been the catalyst for the growth mindset work in the district. She developed a visual framework for school culture (see Figure 12) based on the four components, or pillars, of growth mindset that were introduced in Chapter 2.

The foundation of the framework is a "Safe & Secure Learning Environment." This goes beyond the physical safety of staff and students. It focuses on this question: *Do students and staff feel comfortable and safe taking risks and making mistakes without judgment from others?* FCPS realizes that this must be the foundation for growth mindset work. FCPS teachers are encouraged to model risk-taking in the classroom so that the students will observe and then follow. School leaders and district staff are encouraged to innovate and be bold in their consideration of new strategies, possibilities, and ways to move the school system forward. This foundation speaks to an atmosphere of mutual respect where educators get to know students individually while valuing and respecting cultural differences. The foundation also includes cultivating an environment that encourages creativity and intellectual risk-taking. Teachers and administrators are encouraged to discuss, disagree, and reach consensus with a growth mindset perspective.

The next level in the foundation is "Challenging Curriculum & Engaging Instruction." Earlier in this book I presented a case for productive struggle and why challenge is important to all students. Many of our students are underchallenged. Therefore, providing challenging curriculum and engaging instruction is the goal for all FCPS students. Some of the tenets at this level include productive struggle, formative assessment, and differentiated/responsive instruction. Other components include routine use of preassessments across content areas and flexible grouping providing support and scaffolding at every level. This foundational goal guides the school system's development and implementation of curriculum guides, resources, and assessments. Curriculum specialists and teacher content writers take

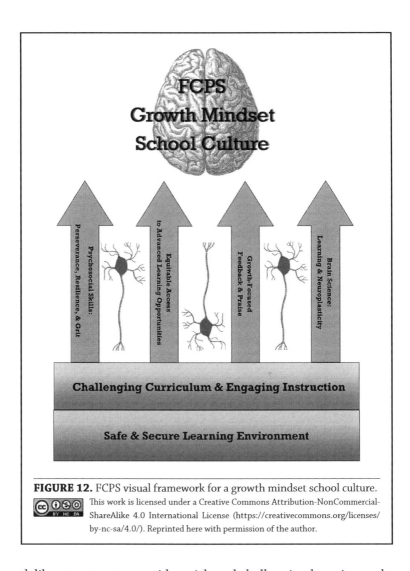

FIGURE 12. FCPS visual framework for a growth mindset school culture.

deliberate steps to provide a rich and challenging learning pathway for students at all levels.

Professional Learning

The Professional Learning plan for FCPS spanned several years. Meg began by facilitating workshops and presentations for her own team of advanced academics and magnet teachers. The sequence of training was as follows:

1. Advanced academics and magnet teachers.
2. Principals and curriculum specialists.
3. Assistant principals.
4. Teacher leader representatives from each elementary, middle, and high school.
5. Business services groups—human resources, maintenance, finance, etc.
6. Support personnel.

Additionally, professional learning was provided at individual schools that wanted to go deeper into understanding the positive impact of mindsets in schools. Many principals began their own school-based professional learning about mindsets, which allowed them to customize the message for the unique needs of their level and building. Several schools implemented "Mindset Mondays," complete with classroom challenges and videos from the principal as part of the morning announcements. Others facilitated book studies and collaborative conversations. One FCPS leader, Eric Rhodes, actually asked a friend to build a backward bicycle that was used during workshops to demonstrate neuroplasticity. If you are not familiar with "The Backwards Brain Bicycle," it is a must-see (visit https://www.youtube.com/watch?v=MFzDaBzBlL0).

Several schools held growth mindset parent events as well. The FCPS Advanced Academics team also developed online modules that can be accessed by teachers at any time. Principals are encouraged to use them on districtwide professional learning days. What a great model for personalized professional learning. The module topics include:

> › Psychosocial Skills: Perseverance, Resiliency, and Grit
> › Equitable Access to Advanced Learning Opportunities
> › Brain Science: Learning and Neuroplasticity
> › Growth-Focused Feedback and Praise
> › Developing a Growth Mindset School Culture

Meg and her Advanced Academics team also wrote a course using a book study model with *Mindsets in the Classroom: Building a Growth Mindset Learning Community* (Ricci, 2017). This course was approved by the Maryland State Department of Education. Teachers who enrolled in the book study course received credit (that could go toward certification renewal) for participation. Superintendent Alban also hosted an online book club that staff, parents, and community members participated in.

Teacher leader representatives, as well as administrators, engaged in a growth mindset school culture self-assessment tool during their professional learning sessions (see Figure 13). This provided an opportunity for them to take what they learned back to their schools to determine a baseline or starting point for the areas that they needed to focus on in their building. This tool can also be used to measure growth in the areas the school team identified as areas of focus.

FCPS uses Charlotte Danielson's Framework for Teaching and Evaluation (The Danielson Group, 2017). The Advanced Academics team completed a crosswalk between the Danielson Framework and the FCPS School Culture Framework. Meg shared the following about the overlap of these two frameworks:

> We were happy to find so many areas where Danielson's Framework for Teaching (the foundational document for our district's teacher evaluation system) was a perfect complement to the FCPS Growth Mindset School Culture Framework. The Framework for Teaching brought to the forefront discussions about the importance of focusing on the students and

Frederick County Public Schools Growth Mindset School Culture
Self-Assessment

Directions: Place a checkmark in the appropriate column to indicate the strength of your agreement or disagreement with each statement. Think about each statement *in the context of your whole school practice*.

SAFE AND SECURE LEARNING ENVIRONMENT

Safe & Secure Learning Environment	Need Strongly Disagree	Disagree	Agree	Strongly Agree	Strength Don't Know
1.1 Classrooms are collaborative learning communities and students are comfortable taking academic risks.					
1.2 Students share challenges and examine mistakes openly.					
1.3 Teachers are encouraged to take risks and try new strategies.					
1.4 Teachers promote growth-focused dialogue about challenges and mistakes.					
1.5 Students are encouraged to ask questions.					
1.6 Mutual respect and trust between students and staff is evident.					
1.7 Students know where to go to access help when they are struggling.					

CHALLENGING CURRICULUM & ENGAGING INSTRUCTION

Challenging Curriculum & Engaging Instruction	Need Strongly Disagree	Disagree	Agree	Strongly Agree	Strength Don't Know
2.1 Teachers can define rigorous instruction in their content/grade level.					
2.2 Rigor is evident in classroom expectations and tasks.					
2.3 Teachers use higher level questioning techniques and students ask their own higher level questions.					
2.4 A high level of student engagement is evident across the school.					
2.6 Students have opportunities to explore their passions and interests and make real-world connections.					
2.7 Teachers differentiate instruction based on pre-assessment.					
2.8 Students enjoy coming to school each day.					

FIGURE 13. FCPS growth mindset school culture self-assessment.

their levels of engagement and agency in the classroom. The Growth Mindset School Culture Framework components help us to focus on providing rich opportunities for learning, while helping to cultivate students' ownership of their learning and understanding of the brain and how it works. The messages in our classrooms, both from teachers and from students, are grounded

GROWTH-FOCUSED FEEDBACK & PRAISE

Growth-Focused Feedback & Praise	Strongly Disagree	Disagree	Agree	Strongly Agree	Don't Know
3.1 Growth mindset feedback is evident in daily communication with students.					
3.2 Students have opportunities to learn from and analyze mistakes.					
3.3 Students have regular opportunities for reflection on learning and growth.					
3.4 Teachers have regular opportunities for reflection on learning and growth.					
3.5 Students are assessed on process as well as end results.					
3.6 Feedback provided to students is purposeful and specific.					
3.7 Students are given opportunities to improve based on feedback.					
3.8 Praise focuses on the product rather than the person.					
3.9 Students participate in goal setting and student growth is monitored and recognized.					

PSYCHOSOCIAL SKILLS: PERSEVERANCE, RESILIENCE, GRIT

Psychosocial Skills: Perseverance, Resilience, Grit	Strongly Disagree	Disagree	Agree	Strongly Agree	Don't Know
4.1 Students have opportunities for productive struggle.					
4.2 Teachers capitalize on mistakes as opportunities for further learning.					
4.3 Students demonstrate healthy coping skills when faced with challenge, setback, or failure.					
4.4 Teachers model healthy coping skills when faced with challenge, setback, or failure.					
4.5 Students understand the concept of perseverance and can provide examples.					

FIGURE 13. Continued.

in the importance of feedback and praise from a growth-focused perspective. It is also critical that educators also continue to develop their own practice by undertaking a close examination of their own mindsets and how those influence their work with each other and with children and families. Ultimately, Frederick County Public Schools plans to close the achievement gap through deliberate actions based on best practices. We will do so within the framework of our individual and collective growth mindsets. (personal communication, March 13, 2018)

EQUITABLE ACCESS TO ADVANCED LEARNING OPPORTUNITIES

Equitable Access to Advanced Learning Opportunities	Need ⟶ Strength				
	Strongly Disagree	Disagree	Agree	Strongly Agree	Don't Know
5.1 Academic placements are not "sink or swim."					
5.2 Percentage of students from underrepresented populations in advanced learning opportunities mirrors the school's demographics.					
5.3 Children are exposed to rigor and challenging experiences commensurate with their academic abilities.					
5.4 Student behavior does not impact academic placement or options.					
5.5 Student scheduling/placement allows for flexibility when needed.					
5.6 Teachers are familiar with strategies for talent-spotting cognitive strengths.					
5.7 A variety of data points are used to make instructional and placement decisions.					

BRAIN SCIENCE: LEARNING & NEUROPLASTICITY

Brain Science: Learning & Neuroplasticity	Need ⟶ Strength				
	Strongly Disagree	Disagree	Agree	Strongly Agree	Don't Know
6.1 Staff can name at least three parts of the brain and their functions.					
6.2 Staff can explain how neural connections work and how to strengthen them.					
6.3 Staff understand the concept of neuroplasticity and can provide examples.					
6.4 Staff know where to access lessons, articles, and resources related to brain science.					
6.5 Students know the basic parts of their brains and how they work.					
6.6 Students understand how to strengthen neural connections.					

FIGURE 13. Continued.

Frederick County Public Schools formed a partnership with Hood College in Frederick, MD. The partnership offers leadership development opportunities for teachers through the new FCPS Vanguard Teacher Program, which emphasizes four areas of teaching competencies: mindset, instructional technology, teaching practices, and professional learning and networking. The partnership is focusing on mindsets in order to help teachers shift toward new methods of teaching and learning. FCPS and Hood College will collaborate regularly to design, assess, and redesign the courses.

Curriculum and Instruction

An innovative group of teachers travels to schools throughout FCPS to work with students in grades K–2. These Primary Talent Development (PTD) teachers visit classrooms and facilitate lessons focused on growth mindset and critical thinking. The classroom teachers observe these visits carefully so that they can continue the work after the PTD teacher leaves. Classroom teachers utilize the strategies that they observe and learn to recognize potential in all students. These primary students learn about mindsets and neural networking in the brain. It is an amazing thing to see kids explain what happens in the brain when we learn.

The FCPS Department of Career and Technology Education collaborated with the Office of Advanced Academics to develop a course for every grade 6 student. The semester-long course is called *Lab21-Learn, Apply and Build 21st Century Skills*. The first unit in the course is about fixed and growth mindsets, and it includes a mindset self-assessment at the beginning of the unit. Mindsets are referenced throughout the remainder of the course. This course helps students navigate the struggles and academics of middle school. Shelly McGaughey, teacher of *Lab21-Learn, Apply and Build 21st Century Skills*, gave some insight about how teaching this course changed her:

> Adding Growth Mindset to my teaching practices has given me the courage to step outside my comfort zone and prepare 21st-century learners, 21st-century style. Otherwise, this former "old school" teacher may have retired by now! (personal communication, March 15, 2018)

A few of the grade 6 students from the course offered their thoughts as well:

> "Mindset is like a plant. Water it, and it will grow. Neglect it, and it will wither and die." —Cyra

> "Growth Mindset means I can be what I want to be!" —Gracie

> "When you reach the top, look around to pull others up." —Caden

> "Having a growth mindset helps me through the day!" —Rory

Frederick County Public Schools is also participating in an international initiative from the Dana Foundation, the annual Brain Awareness Week, which is designed to promote public awareness of the benefits of brain research. This is a perfect complement to the growth mindset component of conceptualizing what happens in our brains as we learn. During Brain Awareness Week, FCPS:

> ⟩ provides an electronic bank of resources for schools that include brain trivia, bulletin board ideas, and mindfulness resources;
> ⟩ encourages media specialists to create book displays relating to the brain (FCPS even gets public libraries to participate);
> ⟩ uses morning announcements to share brain facts each morning; and
> ⟩ tweets using the hashtag #FCPSBrainWeek to share activities and ideas.

Last But Not Least

Frederick County Public Schools is very cognizant of the messages schools send to children. These message focus on growth, such as in this example from the FCPS (2017) website:

> FCPS recognizes that because "giftedness" is not a static trait, labeling a student "gifted" or "not gifted" can be problematic and inaccurate; therefore, FCPS staff endeavor to match the needs of each individual child with the programmatic components that best fit his or her unique learning needs. (para. 4)

Frederick County Public Schools is looking carefully at processes and procedures through a growth mindset lens, and they recognize that becoming a "Growth Mindset District" requires time and ongoing reflection. The commitment is impressive. The students in FCPS are fortunate to have Dr. Alban, Meg Lee, and a number of education administrators who lead, model, and support this very important work.

Discussion Questions

> Think about some of the things that this large school district has put in place. What practices could you adapt or replicate for your school or district?

> Why is learning about mindsets important when establishing new initiatives like the Vanguard Teacher Program (see p. 104)? Why would FCPS and Hood College plan to "redesign" courses before the program even started?

CHAPTER 11

Final Thoughts

If you have spent a good amount of time and effort toward building a growth mindset culture, then it is now time to evaluate how well you, your school, or your district is doing. How do you monitor and make sure that, in fact, the building or office staff is working toward this goal every day? One way is to establish Look Fors, student and teacher behaviors, as well as learning environment indicators, that you will observe when you walk through any room in the school building (see Figure 14). These behaviors should evidence the building of growth mindset beliefs and practices. Another option is to utilize Professional Learning Communities (PLCs) or Professional Learning Networks (PLNs). These groups should focus discussion around the progress toward a growth mindset culture. Set up alerts online so leaders of PLCs will be notified when new articles or studies are released that focus on neuroscience in education and growth mindset.

"Look Fors" in a Growth Mindset Learning Environment

Expectations

> Teacher believes that all students can achieve at high levels.

> Equitable access to advanced learning experiences exists for all students.

> Students and teachers believe in the ability to develop intelligence: students have a conceptual understanding of neural connections.

Cultivation of Psychosocial Skills/ Noncognitive Factors

> Deliberate instruction/cultivation of perseverance, resiliency, grit, and persistence is ongoing.

> Students are given opportunities to safely struggle (not graded) in order to build neural networks and develop resiliency.

> Instructional strategies that nurture/promote higher level thinking are imbedded in everyday instruction.

Classroom Environment

> A growth mindset class culture is evident—students are not saying "I can't."

> Teacher feedback/praise is based on effort, process, and strategies used.

> Failure is looked at in a positive light. What can be learned from the error or lack of success?

> Grades and scores are not emphasized.

> Students are not "labeled" in the classroom: "gifted," "resource," "ELL," "on-level," etc.

> Students are given opportunities to set their own goals and reflect on the outcome.

FIGURE 14. "Look fors" in a growth mindset learning environment. From *Ready-to-Use Resources for Mindsets in the Classroom: Everything Educators Need for Building Growth Mindset Learning Communities* (pp. 134–135), by M. C. Ricci, 2015, Waco, TX: Prufrock Press. Copyright 2015 by Prufrock Press. Reprinted with permission.

Students Might Be Saying

> I don't understand this yet.
> My neurons are not connecting yet.
> If I practice I will get it.
> I am not going to give up.
> I can feel my neurons connecting.
> Can I try something more challenging?

Teachers Are Saying

> You are not quite there yet, but keep trying/practicing.
> I like the way you persevere/persist through that task.
> Let's think of a new strategy when you try this again.
> I am proud of the way that you struggled through that task.
> "Yet"
> I can see the effort you have put into this and your determination to do this well.
> Can you think of a way to make this more challenging for yourself?

Things Seen in the Classroom

> Visual reminder/triggers to have a growth mindset (e.g., poster, neurons, etc.).
> Students grouped flexibly and working at multiple levels.
> Quotes about perseverance and positive reminders about failure.
> Displayed student work shows corrections, redos, and growth.
> Stickers and displays are effort based.

FIGURE 14. Continued.

Have the PLCs adopt books like *Mindsets in the Classroom* (Ricci, 2017) as book study or book club selections. Reflecting and discussing these readings together will help internalize the concept of mindsets.

Now that you are familiar with growth mindset leadership, think about the attributes that leaders should demonstrate in order to model and lead. Building strong, trusting, positive relationships is first and foremost. Then, ask yourself if you are:

> optimistic,
> supportive,
> open-minded,
> inquisitive,
> resilient,
> flexible,
> trustworthy,
> a focused listener, and
> a risk taker.

Additionally, think about the following:
> Do you embrace growth and continuous improvement? Are you coachable?
> Do you learn and make changes from the feedback of others?
> Are you inspired by others' success rather than threatened or envious?
> Do you compete against yourself, not others?
> Are you comfortable with not being perfect and making errors?
> Do you project enthusiasm and positive energy?
> Do others have a clear understanding of your high expectations?

Remember that all of these attributes can be developed with deliberate practice. To help with that deliberate practice, you might also develop some affirmations that you reflect on each morning—things like:
> When I face a challenge today, I will face it head-on.
> I will learn from others today.
> Instead of saying, "We can't do that," I will say, "How can we do that?"
> When I make a mistake, I will admit it and reflect on what I have learned from it.

Building our own resilient behaviors contributes to dealing with the everyday stress that can occur as a leader. The more our thinking leans toward growth, the better we are able to handle stressful situations. Will there be bumps in the road as you create a growth mindset learning community? Of course, but your perseverance, resiliency, optimism, and toolbox of strategies will help you reach your goal: a growth mindset.

Use of the growth mindset has become a part of our culture at St. Johns Lane Elementary School. Every week begins with Mindset Monday, and students and teachers spend their morning meeting time reviewing a video, a quote, a photo, and/or an example of progress and achievement based on the growth mindset process. You hear our students reflecting on their own efforts by saying "I just haven't learned it yet," or "I'm training my brain," and encouraging their classmates by saying "use your strategies," "keep trying," or "you worked hard." As our teachers discuss student growth and progress during data discussions, they talk about student habits of effort, perseverance, and taking on challenges with positivity, as much, if not more than the actual data. Even our report card comments reference effort, production, risk-taking, and personal goal setting, all a part of the growth mindset.

We have included our entire school community by offering a parent book study and parent seminars on our expectations, and provided opportunities to practice and apply the growth mindset principles. As the principal, I present a review of the growth mindset each year for our parents at Back To School Night and reference the growth mindset in my newsletter messages throughout the year. The growth mindset has been written into our School Improvement Plan as one of our strategies to support student progress and achievement. Our first-year growth mindset students are now fourth graders, and we have seen this positive effort-focused strategy support the continued academic and personal success of our students and staff. Our school culture has changed to include the growth mindset as a part of the fabric of what we do every day at SJLES to recognize and encourage student effort and success.

—Vicky Sarro, Principal,
St. John's Lane Elementary School, Ellicott City, MD

Discussion Questions

> What are some ways that you can keep growth mindset momentum going in your school or office?
> What are some other growth mindset affirmations that you could reflect upon each morning?

References

AccuTrain Corporation. (2018). *What is RCD?* Retrieved from http://www.givemefive.com/what-is-rcd

Allen, R. (2012). Support struggling students with academic rigor: A conversation with author and educator Robyn Jackson. *Education Update, 54*(8), 3–5.

Alrubail, R. (2015). Scaffolding student reflections + sample questions. *Edutopia.* Retrieved from https://www.edutopia.org/discussion/scaffolding-student-reflections-sample-questions

Bloch, H. (2013). Failure is an option: Where would we be without it? *National Geographic.* Retrieved from https://www.nationalgeographic.com/magazine/2013/09/famous-failures

Boaler, J. (2016). *Mathematical mindsets: Unleashing students' potential through creative math, inspiring messages and innovative teaching.* San Francisco, CA: Jossey-Bass.

Clifford, C. (2017). Bill and Melinda Gates turn their annual letter into a valentine celebrating Warren Buffett. *CNBC*. Retrieved from https://www.cnbc.com/2017/02/14/bill-and-melinda-gates-celebrate-warren-buffett-with-a-valentine.html

The Danielson Group. (2017). *The framework*. Retrieved from https://www.danielsongroup.org/framework

Dweck, C. S. (2006). *Mindset: The new psychology of success*. New York, NY: Random House.

Dweck, C. S. (2010). Mind-sets and equitable education. *Principal Leadership, 10*(5), 26–29.

Every Student Succeeds Act, Pub. L. No. 114–95. (2015).

Fox, E. (2012). *Rainy brain, sunny brain: How to retrain your brain to overcome pessimism and achieve a more positive outlook*. New York, NY: Basic Books.

Frederick County Public Schools. (2017). *Advanced academics*. Retrieved from https://www.fcps.org/academics/advacademics

Gerstein, J. (2016). Helping your students learn to reflect on their learning. *TeachThought*. Retrieved from https://www.teachthought.com/learning/helping-students-learn-reflect-learning

Kelley, T., & Kelley, D. (2013). *Creative confidence: Unleashing the creative potential within us all*. New York, NY: Crown.

Learning Forward. (2017). *Vision, mission, beliefs, priorities*. Retrieved from https://learningforward.org/who-we-are/purpose-beliefs-priorities

Lightman, D. (2005). Organisation: Optimism brings positive results to the workplace. *LeaderValues*. Retrieved from https://www.leader-values.com/article.php?aid=456

Lohman, D. F. (2004). Reasoning abilities. In R. J. Sternberg & J. E. Pretz (Eds.), *Cognition and intelligence: Identifying the mechanisms of the mind* (pp. 225–250). New York, NY: Cambridge University Press.

MIND Research Institute. (2016). *Using game-based learning in the classroom to develop productive struggle* [Video file]. Retrieved from https://www.youtube.com/watch?v=0WlP8NNo4CU

Mindvalley. (2018). *Understanding positive and negative energy in people* [Web log post]. Retrieved from https://blog.mindvalley. com/positive-and-negative-energy

Olszewski-Kubilius, P. (2013, October). *Talent development as an emerging framework for gifted education.* Presentation given to Baltimore County Public Schools, MD.

Peters, S. J., Matthews, M. S., McBee, M. T., & McCoach, D. B. (2013). *Beyond gifted education: Designing and implementing advanced academic programs.* Waco, TX: Prufrock Press.

Porter, A. C., Murphy, J., Goldring, E,. Elliott, S. N., Polikoff, M. S., & May, H. (2008). *Vanderbilt assessment of leadership in education: Technical manual (Version 1.0).* Nashville, TN: Vanderbilt University.

Ricci, M. C. (2015). *Ready-to-use resources for mindsets in the classroom: Everything educators need for building growth mindset learning communities.* Waco, TX: Prufrock Press.

Ricci, M. C. (2017). *Mindsets in the classroom: Building a growth mindset learning community* (Rev. ed.). Waco, TX: Prufrock Press.

Ricci, M. C., (2018). *Nothing you can't do!: The secret power of growth mindsets.* Waco, TX: Prufrock Press.

Ricci, M. C., & Lee, M. (2016). *Mindsets for parents: Strategies to encourage growth mindsets in kids.* Waco, TX: Prufrock Press.

Scott, S. (2018). Jo Boaler wants everyone to love math. *Stanford Magazine.* Retrieved from https://medium.com/stanford-magazine/jo-boaler-transforming-math-education-ddc23ab 45158

Seltzer, L. (2014). 6 virtues, and 6 vices, of venting. *Psychology Today.* Retrieved from https://www.psychologytoday.com/ us/blog/evolution-the-self/201404/6-virtues-and-6-vices-venting

Silver, D., Berckemeyer, J. C., & Baenen, J. (2015). *Deliberate optimism. Reclaiming the joy in education.* Thousand Oaks, CA: Corwin.

Smith, D. (2014). This is what Candy Crush Saga does to your brain. *The Guardian*. Retrieved from https://www.theguardian.com/science/blog/2014/apr/01/candy-crush-saga-app-brain

Sousa, D. A., & Tomlinson, C. A. (2011). *Differentiation and the brain: How neuroscience supports the learner-friendly classroom*. Bloomington, IN: Solution Tree.

Tschannen-Moran, M. (2014). *Trust matters: Leadership for successful schools* (2nd ed.). San Francisco, CA: Jossey-Bass.

The Wallace Foundation. (2013). *The school principal as leader: Guiding schools to better teaching and learning*. Retrieved from http://www.wallacefoundation.org/knowledge-center/Pages/The-School-Principal-as-Leader-Guiding-Schools-to-Better-Teaching-and-Learning.aspx

Weil, A. (2011). *Spontaneous happiness: A new path to emotional well-being*. New York, NY: Little, Brown.

Wormeli, R. (2011). Redos and retakes done right. *Effective grading practices, 69*(3), 22–26.

APPENDIX A

Administrator's Mindset Reflection Tool: Answer Key

1. You are observing a math class and are happy to see small-group instruction. As you circulate through the room, you see the teacher working with a group of struggling math students. You notice that the teacher jumps in to support each student as soon as he or she gets stuck. What are you thinking?

   a. I really like how this teacher is providing individual help for these students as soon as they need it.

   b. **I wish she would let them struggle a bit more before helping them.**

   c. I wonder why these students are behind the rest of the class. I need to set up a meeting to discuss.

   Response B is a growth mindset response. Although response A is a good practice, we should be careful about jumping in and overhelping students before they have time to struggle a bit and try to work through a question using their own problem-solving skills. If we help too early, students eventually figure out that they don't have to think too hard about problems because someone will help them.

2. During a preservice day, you are leading a staff meeting to discuss some new initiatives that the district has mandated. What do you do?
   a. Come prepared to the meeting with an implementation plan.
   b. **Encourage staff to ask questions, contribute ideas, and participate in the development of the plan.**
   c. Let staff know that these initiatives were not your idea, but central office says that they need to be implemented, so you will all work together to make sure that happens.

   Response B demonstrates strong growth mindset thinking. As leaders we know that it is often "easier" just to develop plans ourselves and present them to staff. However, allowing team members to participate sends a powerful message about your belief in their abilities to effectively contribute. Response C may be true, but sharing that these are someone else's initiatives communicates that you don't value the initiatives, and therefore, staff should not value them.

3. At each grade level in your school you have a special class or group for gifted learners. A teacher comes to you advocating for a child to join the group even though the child has not met the testing and report card grade criteria. How do you respond?
   a. I am sorry, but if I let him in, I will be setting a precedent for others. Can you imagine what parents would do if they found out?
   b. No, he will slow the other kids down.

c. We have the criteria in place for a reason, and he did not meet the criteria.

d. **Let's give him a trial period of 6 weeks and see how he does.**

Response D is a growth mindset response. All of the other responses are fixed—they put policy and parent reactions above a student's instructional needs.

4. Do you believe that *all* educators can develop their teaching skills with practice and effort from the teacher and support and feedback from an instructional coach?
   a. **Yes**
   b. No

   The growth mindset response is yes!

5. Every year each administrator receives feedback from the educators and staff who are part of his or her team. You recently reviewed the feedback and noticed that several people had concerns about you in the following areas: listening without interrupting and micromanaging their work. How do you respond?
   a. Well, I am responsible for what happens in this building/office, and I am sorry that they consider that micromanaging.
   b. These comments are probably from the people that I have had concerns with—sour grapes!
   c. **I really need to work on letting people speak first before I interrupt. I also need to work on backing off my staff . . . I know they have the capacity and expertise to do their job.**

   Response C is the growth mindset response. It doesn't matter who the feedback came from—if there is a pattern, then it should be reflected upon, and effort should be put forth to improve. Even if just one or two people mention the concerns, they are worth considering. What is interesting about the micromanagement comment is that many leaders are not aware that they do this and would likely disagree, stating that, in fact, they do not micromanage. However, micromanagement is the staff's perception, so a conversation about it should take place with your team. Response A may be accurate, and there may be a few team members who need more guidance, but in general, micromanaging does not build positive relationships or communicate trust and optimism.

6. Do you provide specific feedback to teachers outside of evaluations or formal visits?
   a. **Always**
   b. Occasionally
   c. Not often/Never

   Response A. In a growth mindset school or district, the focus is growth. Therefore, leaders should always provide informal feedback that is observed at any time, not just after formal evaluation visits.

7. A teacher approaches you and asks if he can attend a conference focused on ways to embed technology into instruction. He states that he will pay for the conference himself but would like to have approval to attend, and requests that he does not have to use his sick leave if at all possible. What do you think?
   a. He just wants to get away. He will never implement anything that he learns.
   b. **I am so glad that he is seeking new ways to use technology in his classroom. I will ask him to share what he learns when he returns and find a way that he will not have to use sick leave.**
   c. **The conference looks great. I wonder if I can attend and send a few more teachers as well.**

Both Response B and Response C demonstrate growth mind-set responses. Response C also acknowledges needed growth within yourself as well as your team. If, in fact, the team member has a history of attending conferences without changing any practices, then put a support in place that makes him accountable for the new learning. For example, go through the conference offerings (available online prior to conferences) and select sessions together that he will attend and then share the knowledge with his team. If the goal is for him to learn, grow, and improve his practices, then support might be needed to help him get there.

Planning for Students' Unmet Academic Needs

It is likely that every school has students who have unmet academic needs. What are some ways that we can find students who would benefit from a specific advanced academic service, regardless of how a child is labeled or the classes in which he or she is placed? The inspiration for the following resource, "Guidance Document for Advanced Learning Opportunities: Determining and Planning for Students' Unmet Advanced Academic Needs," is the Advanced Academic Model described in the book *Beyond Gifted Education* (Peters, Matthews, McBee, & McCoach, 2013). The following resource is just one possible way to discuss and determine ways to meet high-potential students' unmet academic needs. I encourage you to customize this guidance document for your own school/district. This should be completed with several educators around the table: classroom teacher(s), administrator, and perhaps a content area department head at the secondary level.

Create a Growth Mindset School

The intention of this resource is to begin a discussion about students who are underchallenged and have unmet needs. If no service, curriculum, or instructional experience exists in your school to meet the students' needs, then the team needs to brainstorm possibilities that may not have previously existed or been offered to students. For example, a middle school student could go to the local high school for an Algebra 2 class, or three fourth-grade students could be brought together from their various classrooms to form an intellectual peer group, and various teachers could work together to meet their advanced academic needs. High school students might be set up with an online course/virtual learning experience, be able to take a class at a local community college, or conduct an independent research project with a community mentor.

Guidance Document for Advanced Learning Opportunities: Determining and Planning for Students' Unmet Advanced Academic Needs

Student: _____ Date: _____

Grade/Content Area: _____

Engagement in Learning

Students who are not sufficiently challenged may be disengaged in learning due to lack of rigor or perceived value of work. Circle the student's engagement using the scale below.

1	2	3	4	5
Disengaged		**Somewhat Engaged**		**Highly Engaged**
Uninterested—sees no value in tasks.		Completes work but sees little value in the experience.		Sees value in learning experiences.

Evidence of Potential Unmet Need(s)

Consider current level of mastery, review standard, and advanced curriculum through the lens of student need(s), and consider differentiation that has already occurred for the student. Discuss the following data:

Preassessment/Diagnostic Data: _____

Formative Assessment Data: _____

Summative/Achievement Data Review: _____

Anecdotal Data: _____

Other Data: _____

Parent Input

_____

_____

_____

From *Ready-to-Use Resources for Mindsets in the Classroom: Everything Educators Need for Building Growth Mindset Communities* (pp. 81–82), by M. C. Ricci, 2015, Waco, TX: Prufrock Press. Copyright 2015 by Prufrock Press. Reprinted with permission.

Observation of Noncognitive Factors (Perseverance/Resiliency/Motivation/Work Ethic)

_____

_____

_____

What Instructional Options Are Available to Help Address Any Unmet Needs?

Possibilities:

> Exposure to advanced academics (with support/scaffolding as needed)
> Instruction of above-grade-level standards within regular class
> On-level standards with deep enrichment/critical thinking opportunities within regular classroom
> Participation in Honors or above-level course(s)
> Cross-class cluster grouping to form intellectual peer group
> Cross-grade grouping to meet content area strength
> Blended or personalized learning opportunity through technology
> Elementary student attending middle school for an advanced class
> Middle school student attending high school for an advanced class
> High school student taking an online college course or attending a local college for an advanced course

Other Services/Programming That Could Occur

_____

_____

_____

What (if Any) Professional Learning Should Occur to Support Teachers With Meeting These Student Needs?

_____

_____

_____

_____

From *Ready-to-Use Resources for Mindsets in the Classroom: Everything Educators Need for Building Growth Mindset Communities* (pp. 81–82), by M. C. Ricci, 2015, Waco, TX: Prufrock Press. Copyright 2015 by Prufrock Press. Reprinted with permission.

APPENDIX C

Introducing Neuroscience in the Classroom

In Chapter 2, the four components of a growth mindset learning community were presented (see p. 19). One of those components is developing a conceptual understanding of neural networking in the brain. Having an understanding of neural networking can significantly increase motivation. In Carol Dweck's (2010) original New York City study, students reported that visualizing neural connections helped them move forward. In my visits to schools, I have often heard students state that they think about the neurons connecting when they are faced with a difficult task or have difficulty understanding a new skill or concept. This does not require going deep into neuroscience—just building a conceptual understanding can increase motivation to succeed. Educators and students must recognize that a new neural pathway is like walking through an unexplored forest for the first time. The more frequently the path is used, the fewer the barriers and obstacles that stand in the way. Eventually a clear path is created. That new path represents a clear understanding of the content being taught.

Neuroscience is not a typical area of study in elementary and middle school curriculum and is not often found in high school science, with the exception of a chapter or two embedded in biology or psychology classes. So how do educators find the time to teach students about their brains? Probably one of the most important things to realize is that this is not about just teaching a few lessons. Brain science is an area that must be revisited and built upon over time. It is about introducing and explicitly teaching students, and then routinely revisiting the concept of malleable intelligence so that students realize that intelligence is not about a fixed number, a grade on a paper, or a report card. Students must understand that intelligence is constantly changing based on effort, perseverance, practice, and the struggle that they put forth.

What are some ways that you can build in lessons about neuroplasticity and neural connects into your curriculum and instruction?

About the Author

Mary Cay Ricci is a lifelong educator. She has taught elementary and middle school and has been an education administrator in two large school districts. She is author of *The New York Times* best-selling education book *Mindsets in the Classroom: Building a Growth Mindset Learning Community*. She has also written *Ready-to-Use Resources for Mindsets in the Classroom*, *Mindsets for Parents* (with Margaret Lee), and *Nothing You Can't Do!: The Secret Power of Growth Mindsets*. She is on the board of directors for the Council for Exceptional Children–The Association for the Gifted (CEC-TAG). She currently provides consulting services, professional learning sessions, and keynotes across the country. Follow her on Twitter @MaryCayR or contact her through her website: http://www.marycayricci.com.